Farewell Britain's Television Queen

Bob Crew

© Copyright 2020 Bob Crew

The right of Bob Crew to be identified as the author of this work has been asserted by him in accordance with the Copyright, Designs and Patents Act 1998.

All rights reserved. No reproduction, copy or transmission of this publication may not be made without express prior written permission. No paragraph of this publication may be reproduced, copied or transmitted except with express prior, written permission, or in accordance with the provisions of the Copyright Act 1956 (as amended). Any person who commits any unauthorized act in relation to this publication may be liable to criminal prosecution and civil claims for damage.

Whilst every attempt has been made to contact the relevant photographic copyright-holders, where some were unobtainable, we would be grateful if the appropriate people would contact us. The opinions expressed herein are those of the author and not of MX Publishing.

Paperback ISBN 978-1-80424-119-6
ePub ISBN 978-1-80424-120-2
PDF ISBN 978-1-80424-121-9

Published by MX Publishing
335 Princess Park Manor, Royal Drive,
London, N11 3GX
www.mxpublishing.com

Cover design by Brian Belanger

ACKNOWLEDGEMENTS

With acknowledgements to the global and British fans of the late Queen Elizabeth II and all who take an intelligent interest in the times in which we live, as well as to the memory of all who were involved in making and telling the history of television in Britain, where the world's first televised images were invented and transmitted, as well as the world's first public service television (of certain interest to avid TV viewers, history buffs and science historians); not forgetting my wife Patricia, for proof-reading the first edition of this book some ten years ago, she who has been a fan of British royals and Queen Elizabeth II in particular since she was a young Anglo-Indian child in the days of the Raj in British India, who also has a notable collection of commemorative coins to prove it! The relevance of this is not to be underestimated, not least because her general knowledge of and passion for British royals far outstrips mine, she who has followed the life and times of the late Queen of England since her televised Coronation in 1952 (when my wife was a young girl of nine going on ten years of age in Allahabad in Northern India).

Acknowledgements are also due to the MX publisher of this little book – Steve Emecz – for pledging that MX will donate £1 per book sold to the Red Cross in the UK that has had the enduring support of the Queen of England right throughout the seven decades of her long reign; during which time Elizabeth II has "supported countless Red Cross appeals for tragedies and disasters" in the long reach to time in the UK and around the world that have also benefited from the Queen's personal donations. Elizabeth II would be pleased indeed with the prospect of yet more donations (large or small) for one of her favourite and most enduring charities.

Equally I would like to acknowledge Brian Belanger for the thoughtful illustration and graphic design of the front cover of this book that captures so very well the black and white 'TV-era feel' of those distant 1950s times when the first official images did not appear in colour on British TV screens before 1969, the very first being on BBC 1 (at midnight!) with a concert from the Royal Albert Hall in London, starring the pop star Petula Cark, of Sound of Music Fame, (for those who could afford the 5,000 English pounds (285 guineas) for a colour TV set).

It was in this black and white 1950s era that Britain's Television Queen was born.

Whilst I never met the late Queen of England, I have had occasion to meet her daughter, Princess Anne, and to help show her round a new business school at the University of London - of which she is the patron and I an alumnus - whilst also featuring the Queen's son and successor, Prince Charles before he became King Charles III upon the death of his mother this month (September 2022), in an interview in my 2003 *Gurkha Warriors* military history book, on account of Charles being Colonel in Chief of Britain's Gurkha Regiment in the UK (for which I also received a personal letter of thanks from Prince Harry when he was at Eton College before his admittance to the Sandhurst Military Academy for his officer training).

So here's to acknowledging these royals also for their respective roles when helping to keep this House of Windsor show on the road, especially Charles and Anne, who will have much more to do, now that Queen Elizabeth II has passed on.

Preface (1)

Chapters

One: The Million-Mile Queen and the Commonwealth (18)

Two: The Queen that Went to the Moon (35)

Three: Inventing Televised Royalty (50)

Four: A Fictional Versus a Factual Queen (79)

Five: Britain's Television Decade (104)

Six: Inventing the First Family Reality-TV Show (107)

Seven: A Queen that Puts Her Stamp on the World (124)

Eight: The Queen of England as Television Icon (135)

Nine: Attitudes to Britain's Television Queen (152)

Ten: Is British Royalty Good Value for Money? (158)

Eleven: Rites of Passage for Britain's Television Queen (167)

Twelve: Reasons for the Queen of England's Popularity (175)

Thirteen: Different Audiences for Television Queen (182)

Fourteen: Prominent People and the Queen England (198)

PREFACE

The sequence of events and date-order of the second edition of this book that was first published ten years ago in 2012 is already out of date by a decade – the last of the seven decades of the late Queen of England – and readers need to remember this when travelling back in time to recapture it all. The events and their dates are as they were ten years ago in the past (but written in the present tense of the past when the Queen still had a future) – with the past reading today as if it were the present! - most chapters of which in these present-day pages have not been re-edited or re-written, so their authenticity remains unaltered, as we push at the boundaries of telling history in this way.

Whilst earlier this year (2022) is the time that Queen Elizabeth II of the House of Windsor in England completed 70 years of service to the British people on February 6th when she was still very much alive, at the time of going to press with this second edition of her *Television Queen* book, she is alas, now dead (reminding us that time and tide waits for no man or woman, royal or otherwise!).

When the Queen tested positive for the lethal coronavirus earlier this year - that is, as we know, sadly killing older people in particular because their fragile age makes them especially vulnerable to this wretched condition, long or short – there was no official suggestion from her doctors that she was dying from it or would do so.

Given that the Queen had tested positive – in February of this year – we can see that the ominous month of February has and had turned out to be a recurring fateful-month indeed for her and her late father; and although her palace doctors reported that she was only suffering and being treated for "mild cold-like symptoms" that permitted her to continue with "light duties," the fact remains that this has been, for sure, a pesky fly in the ointment for her remaining health and longer-term strength for her planned Platinum Jubilee celebrations.

As we can imagine, having spent February 6th quietly contemplating the memory of her father (George V1) - who died of lung cancer on this date back in 1952 (he was a heavy cigarette smoker), which is when she officially ascended to his throne - the Queen had not, of course, been in celebratory mood on account of her record-breaking 70 years of service (she was the first and only British monarch to have achieved this), which is why she planned a grand celebration of this later on in the year – in the summer month of June in expectation of warmer and kinder weather, with a week-long Platinum Jubilee event and an unexpected bank holiday for all workers in the UK on account of it.

This virus health problem was no little storm in a royal teacup, but extraordinary drama that was for real; not yet a crisis, but certainly for real, and now, as we know, she has sadly died at 96 years of age, but not of the virus, by all accounts (the palace has played the virus down while mysteriously not confirming what she has died from!).

Was it cancer or some other killer oldie-disease and why the mystery?

Not being immune to the accursed corona virus that is afflicting and/or threatening and jeopardising so many of us - especially at her great and fragile age of 96 years – Queen Elizabeth II also became the first British monarch to test positive of this lethal condition, if not the first queen anywhere in the world to do so, just as this book may very well be the first to record and lament this so promptly after her death, so there is a triple whammy here, not merely a double one, as follows: (1) The queen remembered the sad death of her late father in the month of February (2) It was announced that she caught the coronavirus in the month of February (3) She also became the first monarch to do so in the month of February.

Whilst she will be remembered for other things besides television, it seems to me that the sparkling jewel in her crown in the 20th and 21st centuries has certainly been television, as we shall discover in these pages on this sad occasion of her recent death, and this will almost certainly be the only book to record this for history and for those with an eye for the more unusual and revealing things about her and the significance of her reign, the full history of which is often lost on the populist mainstream media and publishing industry.

As we shall see, she has been much more than a fairy-tale Queen in her ivory tower and not least a very democratic queen, and it is worth noting that, in the most recent *Democracy Index* compiled by the Economist Intelligence Unit in London, six out of the top ten democracies in the world – and nine of the top 15 – are all monarchies, including five Continental European monarchies -Norway, Sweden, Denmark, Netherlands, and Luxembourg - and also Britain, of course, off the coast of Continental Europe.

This was at the last count in 2020 and reported in September of that year. Not only has Queen Elizabeth democratised her monarchy much more than previously, her monarchy may have democratised Britain more as well, by reason of the time-honoured and matured (like a vintage classic wine) constitutional interaction and subtle consultation required in the exercise of power between government and monarchy. Whilst this book is not the place to explore or ague the pros and cons of this – another book for another time perhaps – it is hard to deny, from the findings of the *Democracy Index*, that a constitutional monarch is a good rather than a bad thing for the exercise of presidential or prime ministerial power in a democratic country/world and, as we know, there are some republican presidents and prime ministers who have debauched, abused and perverted the power that they have had and rendered it much less rather than more democratic (the former President Trump of the United States comes readily to mind, as does the former Prime Minister Boris Johnson in the UK, to mention but two of the great democratic powers of the world, and it is furthermore interesting to note that in the United States the Queen of England has a 60% approval rating for the popularity of British royals there where she has been much more popularly approved than any other royal).

And if anyone doubts the *Democracy Index* of the Economist Intelligence Unit (by the *Economist* magazine in London), go google it and discover what a very credible and worthy index it is.

Whilst there are those who think that monarchy is wrong in principle, we live in a paradoxical world in which a lot of wrong things come good and eventually work well if not very well in practise – including democracy itself that is right in principle but not always good in practise! – and this is an argument that also applies to the religions of this world, is it not?

When applied to the late Queen Elizabeth II, working well in practise is what she has definitely achieved by any standard of any democratic monarchy or democratic or undemocratic democracy. With common consent, she has been one of the best – if not the very best in the world – to work well for her people, serving them honestly, cleanly and diligently, exactly as she has been required to do, and how many republican and other presidents or prime ministers can say that?

Of course, she has had an easier ride than politicians – she only needs to be everywhere for her people and comfort them, looking good and smiling well and caringly telling them what they want to hear – so hers has not been mission impossible by any means, as not infrequently is the impossibly bumpy ride of politicians, and for obvious reasons, as we all know only too well. She has had only one all-important task, while they have and have had several with so many banana skins on which to slip up and fall on their faces!

She has only had to say 'I love you all,' while they have had to say 'we are going to tax you, fine you, make you redundant or unemployed, send you to war or to hell and back,' etc, etc, etc !!

There are, of course, already numerous books about Queen Elizabeth II's massively-overdone and over-hyped life and times and royalist inheritance, for those that follow her royal footsteps at every twist and turn, but there is not a single book about her pioneering role as Britain's and the World's television queen, which is why this second edition of this ten year old book is back in circulation again; the first edition having been published in London in 2012 by MX Publishing for the occasion of her Diamond Jubilee.

Queen Elizabeth II was the second-only Diamond Queen since Queen Victoria in the 19th century to have reigned for more than 60 years (Elizabeth in the 20th and 21st centuries) and to enjoy a Diamond Jubilee celebration (as it happens, my un-crowned wife and I have also celebrated our own 'Diamond Wedding Reign,' so we do understand the drift and drag of a long haul, which is not to be underestimated however romantically or platonically 'in love' one may have the good fortune to be).

When the British establishment turned out in force for this second-only Diamond Jubilee ten years ago, so, too, did the pop music establishment with the famous Beatle, Sir Paul McCartney, Tom Jones, Cliff Richard and Elton John, all cheerfully singing for their Diamond Jubilee Queen and with Paul McCartney typically making his famous/infamous quip about the fans (reportedly at least 10,000 of them ticketed) needing to "leave in an orderly fashion" if they did not want Her Majesty to "unleash the corgis" on them!

He did not finish up in the Tower of London!

Nothing testified more visually and with greater impact in the modern age - than this Diamond Jubilee party - to Queen Elizabeth II's image as a very popular television queen, and as we shall see later in this preface, Paul McCartney won a Queen Elizabeth II Coronation Prize when she first ascended to her throne when he was still a schoolboy (as did I, as it happens) and by 1969 he had already recorded a song for her entitled *Her Majesty* (an Abbey Road album from which the other Beatles were notably conspicuous by their absence on the sound track!).

Such was the power of television lighting effects and trick photography that Buckingham Palace had the visual image of a council estate block of flats superimposed upon it during all the Diamond Jubilee fun and games, with reference to *Our House* song!

But long before her Diamond Jubilee – by some 60 years - the late Queen Elizabeth II had been the first and only British monarch to allow a royal coronation to be fully televised – inside London's Westminster Abbey (in 1953) where the TV cameras had previously been disallowed for such a purpose – and this was when I was a 13/14-year-old schoolboy and she was 25 years of age, as I watched her and her coronation on my parents' television set in my home in Reading in Berkshire in the Southeast of England - some 40 miles west of London by road (lower middle-class and working-class relatives and neighbours came running to watch this history-making event with us because they did not yet have television sets of their own back then, so it was a very crowded room!) - and we watched it on a television set not unlike the one shown on the cover of this book.

To mark the occasion of her Coronation, Queen Elizabeth II launched her Coronation Prize, regionally throughout the UK for 'public spirited' school children who had distinguished themselves, not only the classroom, but (more importantly) in the community as well: and as it happens I won this award in Reading and Berkshire for having achieved all my house colours at school for the mainstream sports, representing my school in the community regionally and also nationally (the latter for cross country running), whilst also writing and acting in two school plays for parents and other members of the local community (and being top of my class for good measure in a goodly number of subjects).

In my experience and speaking/writing from memory, one had to work really hard to win this prize and to be an overachiever, and the prize that I received was two books from the WH Smith book shop in Broad Street Reading in the centre of town, with the Queen's head embossed in gold on the front cover of each, and with a certificate labelled inside the front cover of each declaring me a winner of this royal award.

I chose each book for myself - *One Hundred Great Lives* (about the most famous political, military, literary and other people, including explorers, throughout history) and also an *Oxford University Travel Atlas* (with detailed and coloured maps for all the different parts of the UK, for all my long-distance cycling holidays and weekends all over the country staying at Youth Hostels and typically cycling 80/100 miles daily to different destinations, including some abroad in Germany and Belgium.

The National Cross Country Schoolboy Championship in which I represented my county – Berkshire – was at Heaton Park, Manchester, in the North of England, up a unrelentingly steep hill for several miles!

And this, too, was televised.

Needless to say, young schoolboys were proud indeed to have won a Queen Elizabeth II Coronation Prize, for which this new Queen and the local educational authorities had searched the entire country at the grass roots to discover how many outstanding prize winners there were.

Clearly, the young Queen Elizabeth II was a very inspirational and imaginative new queen with obvious leadership qualities and this accounted for a lot of her widespread popularity – for sure she will be a hard act to follow now that she has died - she who had the common touch, like no other, as very sensibly recommended to those in power and/or aspiring to power by the very late $19^{th}/20^{th}$ century poet, novelist and journalist, Rudyard Kipling, as follows:

"If you can keep your head when all about you
    Are losing theirs and blaming it on you,
If you can trust yourself when all men doubt you,
    But make allowance for their doubting too;
If you can wait and not be tired by waiting,
    Or being lied about, don't deal in lies,
Or being hated, don't give way to hating,
    And yet don't look too good, nor talk too wise:

If you can dream—and not make dreams your master;
    If you can think—and not make thoughts your aim;
If you can meet with Triumph and Disaster
    And treat those two impostors just the same;
If you can bear to hear the truth you've spoken
    Twisted by knaves to make a trap for fools,
Or watch the things you gave your life to, broken,
    And stoop and build 'em up with worn-out tools:

If you can make one heap of all your winnings
    And risk it on one turn of pitch-and-toss,
And lose, and start again at your beginnings

   And never breathe a word about your loss;
If you can force your heart and nerve and sinew
   To serve your turn long after they are gone,
And so hold on when there is nothing in you
   Except the Will which says to them: 'Hold on!'

If you can talk with crowds and keep your virtue,
   Or walk with Kings—nor lose the common touch,
If neither foes nor loving friends can hurt you,
   If all men count with you, but none too much;
If you can fill the unforgiving minute
   With sixty seconds' worth of distance run,
Yours is the Earth and everything that's in it,
   And—which is more—you'll be a Man, my son! ''

    Whilst I of course have no idea if Queen Elizabeth II was very familiar with this poem (of which she will certainly have heard) - or warmed to it very much or even at all, -it nevertheless strikes me as a poem that characterizes some of her very obvious best and most memorable qualities, so it is included therefore in this preface for the historical record.

    I discovered in more recent years that, in Liverpool (not too far from the aforesaid Heaton Park in Manchester), this other young aforesaid schoolboy - of whom I had not heard in those distant times - had also won a Queen Elizabeth II Coronation Prize in that city, by the name of the aforementioned Paul McCartney, before he became a famous pop star, winning this prize for, among other things, writing an award-winning essay about Britain's exciting new queen back in 1952 and 1953.

Inevitably this is a book that is breaking new ground as Queen Elizabeth II passes on, leaving all the old ground and old books behind her, this book being the only one – a slim volume simply told for quick and easy reading – on the subject of why the late queen will or should be remembered most of all (in my opinion), as Britain's television queen; and this is because she has existed for her people more powerfully and more visibly on their television screens than anywhere else – and has continued to do so to this day, of course - having gone out of her way to invite the television cameras into her life, at the expense of losing much if not most of her royal mystique.

Prompted by her late husband, HRH Prince Philip, the late Duke of Edinburgh, she has moved with the times and also ahead of the times where television has been concerned, but she has not been given sufficient credit for this, as she is given in these pages.

On the contrary, she has too often been perceived as one who has been harassed and given no peace by television and the rest of the media, with which she has reluctantly come to terms, regarding it at best as a necessary evil.

But when we look at the facts, we see that the reverse is true, that she has very willingly embraced television from the outset of her reign (and why should she not?).

For sure, television has been a double-edged sword, but that has not deterred her from wielding it in her best interests.

This book is written in order to demonstrate this, for the interests, not only of royalists and the fans of British royals, but for all who take an intelligent interest in the times in which we live, and in the role of the media and royalty to that end.

So this is a book for general readers as well as royalists and the fans of royalty, for avid TV viewers and history buffs (concerning contemporary history and the science and history of television).

When this book was first published to mark the late Queen's Diamond Jubilee in 2012, American, European, Commonwealth and other tourists were pouring into London for obvious reasons, as was the world's media in order to cover the Queens' mega-party celebrations, which is why my book was published, of course, and not least for those in the media interested to know about the television phenomenon that was and always had been Britain's television queen (even media studies students and their lecturers sat up and paid attention).

And my publisher and I were not wrong about the media interest, because I finished up on Ukrainian Television for one hour, being interviewed about Britain's television queen for millions of viewers in Ukraine (that is in the grim news now, as we know, for less celebratory matters, alas and alack).

I have a recording of this interview in the Ukrainian language in which I can recognise my face but not my voice!

The interview took place in the National Liberal Club in Whitehall in London – of which I am a life member, but not a political member of that club – just across the road and round the corner from 10 Downing Street and also just across the River Thames facing Big Ben in the tower of the parliamentary House of Commons.

This club was ideal tor Ukrainian Television on the subject of Britain's television queen – traditional and rather splendid classically English décor, great views down the River Thames and of nearby Parliament and Big Ben, uninterrupted quiet for interviewing purposes, female members as well as male, nice and homely relaxed atmosphere (not too formal).

What more could these television guys need?

For reasons of public interest, the distinction is made in these pages between royalists and fans of royalty, with the former being those who consider themselves 'born' royalists – die-hard patriots who have been born into staunchly royalist families, perhaps for generations – and others who have become fans without being born royalists or staunchly royal, but both considering British royalty as a class-act and good idea that is preferable to republicanism.

And this is a distinction that is made for both kinds of reader and/or television viewer, there is room for both and public interest for both, whether as book for book-worms or television viewers/newspaper readers.

The world is indeed a stage on which we all have our parts to play – to quote the inimitable bard – lumbered as we are by our history and best traditions and customs that have their continuing parts to play for the better in this rich tapestry of life in which we find ourselves; and with a history that is arguably very much for the better in the argument of this publication, thanks in no small part to television keeping us all informed and on our toes, and not least our political, royal and religious leaders on their toes likewise, as they clean up their act and know where's it's at, as we shall see before we are through with this book.

Whilst the best of British television spreads the word, gives praise where it's due (and quite right too), doing its best to give everyone a voice - it also asks the difficulty questions, investigates and exposes what is wrong and/or bad in society (*BBC Panorama and also Channel Four* as well as documentaries/politically sensitive interviews all come to mind, as do the *BBC's Reality and Fact Checks*) – so it is a movable feast that is predictably the envy of the world, as one has to admit is British royalty (that is occasionally at loggerheads with the television to which it owes so much!).

This does not mean of course that television does not have its faults or occasionally get things wrong or not quite right and this is also delivered to our TV screens sooner or later.

Whilst I am not a media studies or history graduate, I am an investigative journalist and Eng Lit graduate of the University of London (who switched from the study of law) who knows his culture, media and historical corridors of power well enough, to have no doubt about the political, social and cultural value of British television.

We need the transparency of our television and print media – and also the best of our updated traditions – to get the best out of our leaders and those that vote for them, our power brokers and public opinion influencers. We need and have them all in a reasonable balance in the UK, which is why we don't' need any *group think* or any *cancel culture think*. On the contrary we need all points of view and to let everything come out in the wash, as it usually does, sooner or later, one way or another, airing our dirty linen in public, royal or other dirty linen.

And whether we and the foremost British royals like it or not, they are these days all media icons of one kind or another and this is as a result of Queen Elizabeth II embracing television as she has, for the reasons that she has.

But this is not at all how things were when she first came to her throne in 1952, since when the face of British broadcasting, royalty and society at large has been changed beyond all recognition. It has been changed not least by Queen Elizabeth agreeing to her 1953 coronation being televised –when her advisors were warning her against the big bad television beast – as well as her agreeing to other television programmes besides.

One suspects that it goes against the grain with a goodly number of traditional royalists that today's royals appear to be mere television icons much of the time, but on the other hand, a greater number of fans are well pleased with their royals as TV-icons, since it is through their familiarity with them as the populist icons they have become on their television screens that they have become fans.

That Queen Elizabeth II and Buckingham Palace have had no serious problem with this is suggested by the fact that they have largely willingly gone along with it all in order to stay in touch with the greatest number of people, not just their royalist admirers, but the public at large among whom they have so many more admirers.

All this gives rise to such questions as:

Where would British television be today without its royals to boost its ratings with millions of extra viewers (not so much those who view the news but others viewing the programmes about British royals)?

How would TV look today without a regular royal presence on our screens?

How do British royals compare with other TV-icons?

These are chief among the questions addressed in this book.

As one who has lived through these times and spent the greater part of his adult life in the media – and also had some previously limited experience as already mentioned of royals (HRH Prince/King Charles, HRH Prince Anne the Princess Royal, not forgetting Prince Harry) - I can address these and other questions in these pages not without with some authority.

In the media I have been a correspondent for *The Times* and *Financial Times* and, as already mentioned, I have interviewed Prince Charles in a military history that I have written about Britain's Gurkha soldiers now in its third edition.

As we shall see in chapter two, I first wrote about British royals when I was *The Times* correspondent in Saudi Arabia in the 1970s where Queen Elizabeth was advised by the British ambassador in Jeddah and subsequently her foreign secretary to stay on her royal yacht during a state visit to the desert kingdom because of the Saudi's 'undignified handling of women.'

I broke this story long before my Gurkha book featuring Prince Charles in 2003.

And when I was presented to Princess Anne as one of a reception committee that showed her round a newly-opened business school premises at the University of London, of which she is Chancellor and I am a member of Congregation (she also presented my daughter Michele with her University of London MA degree in the Royal Albert Hall) – in conversation with Anne on that University of London occasion I gained some fleeting but useful insights into her personality, attitudes and character, as we shall see in chapter four.

These, then, are my credentials and reasons for writing this book and the background against which I have written it, as the popular royal and contemporary television history book that it is, principally for lay readers that I hope will also be an informative and enjoyable engaging read for royalists and others besides.

Probably this book is the first draft of Queen Elizabeth II's television history, as I can find no other on this subject.

Bob Crew, BA (Hons), MA
Hampstead Garden Suburb,
North London,
September 2022

Chapter One:

The Million-Mile Queen and the Commonwealth

Just as this book is a popular history for a quick and easy read by busy people - with not too much time on their hands for a long and detailed read - so too is this first chapter in particular about the late Queen Elizabeth II and the Commonwealth of Nations that is a huge subject requiring much more scholarly research and study (another book for another time perhaps); which is why this subject was not included in the first edition of this publication ten years ago in 2012 when the story told in its pages was solely and narrowly about her role as a *Television Queen*, rather than as an inevitable political or ambassadorial Queen of foreign affairs (which traditionally and constitutionally has always been correctly disallowed in the UK, at least in theory, if not in practise off-record!).

But on reflection it was the globally televised and highly political and politically sensitive Commonwealth that played a really big and important, ongoing and broader part in the late Queen's televised success as a monarch, as was the way in which she used television for this Commonwealth purpose; so the time is now due if not overdue to acknowledge this in this second edition that is also commemorating and celebrating her death, as it was not ten years ago when there was no talk or thought of her dying.

Because of the increasing and continuing nature and influence of the multi-racial and multi-cultural rollercoaster *phenomenon* called the Commonwealth of Nations - that the late Queen helped to mother and nurture as she bonded with it very personally and pleasurably indeed - because of the increasing and expanding influence and purpose for the good and the better of the Commonwealth since 2012 ten years ago (with today's Commonwealth mourning and commemorating this month's September 2022 death of the Queen, as much as if not more so than the rest of the world)....because of all this, this new chapter is added to these pages for these reasons.

It has been famously and controversially said by several commentators that it has been a big mistake to ignore the late Queen's un-ignorable and very impressive role as a leading ambassador in foreign affairs and not least in Commonwealth affairs (many scholars have traditionally ignored this on account of it having been a traditional no-go area).

In other words, according to royal critics, the Queen really has been (in reality rather than in the mythical world of illusion) an indirect and unofficial very discreet ambassador
extraordinaire not only for the good of her country, but also for the good of the English-speaking Commonwealth countries around the world, so ignoring her quasi-ambassadorial and subtle role in this respect (ignoring this for fairy-tale reasons of political and constitutional correctness, purely because she has also been rubber-stamped as non-political and therefore firmly above and divorced from politics and political opinion and

debate), has, they argue, been an absurd mistake that has not worked convincingly or honestly/credibly well; and this is because intelligently keen observers can of course see through this pretence/illusion, given that they are not children (even though most people have nevertheless been very happy with the Queen in this child-like way, as we have seen from the abundant evidence of this from global television reports both before and after her 2022 death this month).

Of course there are always many different interpretations and opinions of this highly political matter, of which this is only one - different interpretations and opinions among many from royalists, republicans, politicians, diplomats, historians and in the media - but there are a growing number who believe that to ignore her superb and very effective ambassadorial role and skills has been a big and needless mistake (not that they are advocating political activism for monarchs because they certainly are not, they don't want that, they want the best of both worlds, which is what the Queen has given them!).

For example, there are currently royals and others who are very critical of the brilliant and very well acted Netflix television series *The Crown* (about the House of Windsor) which they allege is historically inaccurate with too many 'artistic inventions' and too much literary/fictional licence and too many liberties taken; but the historian who is the consultant to this factional and very intelligent series certainly begs to differ!

He is the highly accomplished, acclaimed and profusely published Cambridge University educated Robert

Lacey- a former Bristol Grammar School boy who married the daughter of the 8th Marquis of Londonderry (Lady Jane, Baroness Rayne) - who is not only very well published but critically well reviewed with it, having researched and written such best-selling books (published in the English-speaking world of course) as: *Majesty: Elizabeth II; God Bless Her; Aristocrats; The Queen Mother's Century; The Queen: A Life in Brief* ; *Inside the Kingdom* [of Saudi Arabia]; *A Brief Life of the Queen; Battle of Brothers* [the princes William and Harry]; *Royals; The Crown: The Official Companion, The Crown: The Inside History; Princess* [Grace Kelly]; *Sir Walter Raleigh; The Life and Times of Henry VII* and so on.

For sure, there are many very different but equally well-informed (apparently) opinions about British royals and their lives and history with which to cloud the issue for the mere mortals who are their readers or TV viewers!

For my money, *The Crown* is excellent television, just as Robert Lacey is an excellent historian and author, and this is a factional drama that does not take too many liberties that are in any way harmful, outrageous or unacceptable to anybody with half a brain. Lacey and the scriptwriters, actors and director have all done an excellent job and have nothing to apologise for. Their critics are forgetting that this is a very reasonable and well-researched work of factional-fiction that we are talking about here. We are not talking about public relations – pubic relations more like! – or propaganda for the House of Windsor that is being far too touchy on this occasion.

Interestingly, the new King Charles III - the late 96-year-old Queens' 73-year-old son and heir and former royal activist well-known for his political and other opinions - when asked if he is ready to give up his activism now that he has become King (as he is constitutionally pledged to do), has replied, "of course I am, I am not that stupid."

So why be stupid about other things about the House of Windsor that we all know have gone wrong and object to them when they are turned into fiction/faction?

Nor was the King's mother that stupid with regard to her opinions that remained silently tight-lipped (as she dropped her hints and charmed her people instead, with her smiley face and very colourful and stylish designer-clothes).

But what, in brief, has been the late Queen's relationship with and responsibilities for the truly extraordinary Commonwealth of Nations featured in this chapter?

Ever since she acceded to her throne in February 1952 at 25 years of age - following the death of her father, George VI, 70 long years ago - she became Head of the Commonwealth with a hands-on leadership position of challenging responsibility that was not an hereditary one (so she was not obliged to accept it, just as its members were not obliged to accept her, and the same has been and remains the case for her 2022 successor-son, King Charles III, now that his mother has sadly died at the ripe old age of 96 years).

But accede to her Commonwealth role is exactly what she did, with inter-racial and multicultural enthusiasm, relish, passion, goodwill and vigour back in 1952 (all of which was excellent for improved race relations from there on, albeit not without difficulties large and small along the bumpy way, of course, it's the way of the world, is it not?).

This was when she was young and inexperienced, with a little toddler-Commonwealth of only a handful of territories on her hands that was already in existence and in need of more shape and form, continuity and unity in the years ahead (already in existence for three years previously under her father when a so-called *London Declaration* had been signed with great foresight for the Commonwealth's development, with free and equal membership between its member states/nations); pre-existing in this way before the Queen stepped onto the world stage, pre-existing as a small multicultural body of only eight former territories of the British Empire that became independent nations in their own right - so it was no more than a seedling germ of a futuristic and far-sighted, very good idea, a little acorn that was not as yet the oak tree that it has become today.

This is how it was, way back, when the Queen of England entered into its affairs, nothing more than an idea about a small group that had not grown into the astonishing 56 countries that it has become today (representing a staggering one third of the world's population!), after 70 years of the Queen's careful and caring nurturing that has attracted so many countries to its ranks and kept most of them happy (with relatively few defections and suspensions).

Most of these territories and/or countries were (but not all and not necessarily) former British Empire countries and/or territories from the days of the British Raj, and this clearly shows (does it not?) that there has been no irreparable or lingering hard feeling, anti-royal or anti-British feeling (racially, political or otherwise) in the post-colonial and modern world about those distant colonial times (otherwise there would be no Commonwealth to this day where the late Queen remained head of state in 14 of them).

It also shows that Britain and the Queen have been nurtured in return by this extraordinary Commonwealth as much as they nurtured it - with a lot of mutually beneficial nurturing and understanding for each other going on, as the two sides of the same multicultural, human-rights, trade and historical coin have very sensibly and inevitably put the past behind them and learned from each other (including learning from past mistakes), moving on from their past in a genuine spirit of racial goodwill and camaraderie.

In the same way that Germany, France and Britain have put World War Two behind them and moved on, so the Commonwealth Nations and Britain have moved on. What else or what better could they do or have done, as they have paid the price for their respective histories and moved on?

All this Commonwealth stuff followed on from past times when the jewel in Britain's crown of empire was of course India (and Pakistan), and the two biggest white Commonwealth territories/countries were Canada and Australia as they still are the biggest political powers today.

But these two and Britain are no longer the biggest Commonwealth economies today - on the contrary, the economic Commonwealth jewel in the crown has gone to India, followed by Britain, Canada, Australia and Nigeria in this economic order. So times are certainly changing and evolving and these Commonwealth nations could have done a lot worse.

And this infant Commonwealth to which the late Queen acceded has had a lot of shaping-up and growing-up to do as well as a lot of renewal to do, as it has taken a new and better shape under the late Queen's and its own influence and not least from Britain's parentage and nurturing - from a Queen so young and also inexperienced, to begin with back then, she who has been the longest-serving Queen of England in history and has shaped-up with and for her Commonwealth and its people, for the long-term better.

This has been a parentage that could have gone badly wrong so easily (as all parentages can and do, as we know, and as Queen Elizabeth II knew perfectly well from her own family with all its televised and very fractious personal and sexual problems, she who once said that "grief is the price that we pay for love," and who did not instantly identify and agree with that?).

And had she not kept her eye on the ball and nurtured her relatively new-born Commonwealth babe in the years ahead with loving care, attention to detail and sensitivity, not forgetting her winning smile (from the heart not the head) - a toddler-babe that adopted and kept faith with her with unrivalled multiracial and multicultural enthusiasm and goodwill - the chances are that the Commonwealth could not and would not have demonstrated that postcolonial Britain was in no way or no longer set to be formally racist or colour prejudiced in the post-colonial world, for as long as she had anything to do with it; given that Britain really had acknowledged that it was pay-back time for the former British Empire.

In the historical circumstances, she and her country could do no more than that, and *that* is was it did so very well indeed, so a big feather in her cap for this, for Britain having finally bitten the bullet and done the decent thing, as well as for her helping to nurture all these countries of different black, white, yellow and brown plumage with tact, diplomacy and sensitivity (and very hard work and gruelling travel by land, sea and air) into a family of nations, thereby earning and winning their respect for the gracious, considerate, gentle and caring way in which she did this with an unaccustomed lightness of touch and such excellent good conduct, humour and affection, the very least that was required.

Not only had the Commonwealth come of age during her reign, but Britain and its royals and she had come of age likewise, with the two sides complimenting each other remarkably well, and with such an excellent opinion of her in virtually all Commonwealth countries.

When I wrote my Nelson Mandela book nine years ago in 2013 - *Mandela: His Life and Legacy for South Africa and the World,* published in New York by Skyhorse who observed that "Crew gets to the truth and unexpected details of Mandela and current South African president Jacob Zuma" - one of the details I was pleased to discover from Mandela and quote him for saying was that the British were, in his opinion, always "more far sighted" racially, diplomatically and politically than other white nations.

Which is why, as a black man and founder-president of an independent and democratic South Africa (that took over from the odious apartheid of white minority Dutch-Afrikaner rule in that white racist county), he had more confidence in the Brits to do the right and just, humane and decent thing, than in other former empire colonisers that were not far-sighted in this respect; some of whom disgraced themselves big-time when their empires came so acrimoniously and grudgingly to an end, as we know from the historical records.

Old and new generations of Brits really had learned their lessons and reformed and redeemed themselves in contrast to other white racists who had not done so.

To be far-sighted (and insightful) in this tricky-dicky, wicked world, is no easy task on the slippery slope of world and home affairs - either for political, military and religious leaders, or otherwise for royals - but far-sighted and insightful is exactly what the late Queen of England eventually turned out to be (albeit not without dropping a few well-publicised domestic clangers of her own, just like the rest of us, as many if not most families do).

All this and more is chiefly what has endeared the late Queen to her fans at home and abroad and saddened them the more by her loss right now, but they can certainly take comfort from the opinion polls in the UK that tell them that committed republicans in Britain who want shot of their royals are only one-quarter of the population at most, not quite a mere spit in the ocean, but no great threat to constitutional monarchy either, as they eat their hearts out with their 80,000 campaigners who seem to be getting nowhere fast; getting nowhere fast because the Queen was always a compassionate comfort to the people she so diligently served while also working so constantly hard in order to serve them without doubt, to always be there for them without doubt on her ubiquitous walkabouts, workplace visits, care home, school and hospital visits and by supporting their charities without doubt.

Thus far and more recently we have seen democratically elected republican and other presidents and prime ministers disgracing themselves and dishonouring their office - some of whom have made their mark in history as the worst and most dishonest, idle, incompetent, bullying and corrupt ever - but not, as yet, a royal king or queen in the UK, setting their example to and for the world (an occasional prince, certainly, but not a king or queen).

And those that have disgraced themselves have of course and inevitably been in a goodly number of Commonwealth countries, as well as in the Western World.

From 1952/53, the late Queen made some 285/290 state and/or high profile diplomatic visits to Commonwealth and/or other non-Commonwealth countries (these visits have been defined differently in different countries), whilst rubber-stamping (as she is obliged to do) and working with 15 British Prime Ministers at home, from Winston Churchill to Liz Truss today (her favourite British Prime minister was reportedly the Socialist Harold Wilson, and not least because, like her, he not infrequently did his wife's washing-up in their kitchen when he was at home!).

And she has been well-known for doing her politically homework and knowing her constitution inside out in order to master her job both in the UK, the Commonwealth and elsewhere abroad. She has understood and responded competently and responsibly to the affairs of state in the UK, as well as to foreign and Commonwealth affair beyond British shores.

Britain not only has the most successful and well-respected/loved monarchy in the world, but also the longest surviving for 1,000 years (*mein gott!*) going right back to its first Anglo Saxon origins, with the current will and love of its people for their present-day monarchy that clearly works for them, so why fix it if it's not broken (is the attitude of the majority, as they look to their history)?

England's chiefly Saxon founder monarchs (originally from Wessex) have given rise to royals who have done far-sighted deals with other monarchies along the way in the fullness of time – intermarrying with a goodly number – including the Scots later on in more recent history who have been indirectly and directly related to the House of Windsor (as have the Danes and Germans on the late Duke of Edinburgh's side, as well as Prince Albert's Victorian side before that), and it is almost certainly the case that the late Queen's last act of diplomacy has been to take herself off to a death bed in Scotland and die there in the hope of dropping a very large and obvious hint to the Scots that she has always preferred to see them and favour them as a major player in the United Kingdom rather than breaking away from it and becoming independent.

Not that anybody has dare to mention of discuss this during her last days or day of mourning!

But there has been no blood-bath of brutally murdered or massacred royals in the UK for hundreds of years - with heads rolling in recent history - as in other countries, but there has been a 17th-century civil war, of course, between royalist cavaliers and republican round heads, not that the latter lasted for very long when they won this war, because the British soon got fed up with them and welcomed back an exiled king (Charles II)!

For these reasons, Britain has always been a safe haven for royals.

But not for nothing was the 20th/21st century Queen Elizabeth II known as "The Million-Mile-Queen," as well as "The Most Popular Brit Of All Time Since Churchill" and also "The Most Well-Travelled Head of State in History" and she is on record as saying of the Commonwealth that, she always wanted to "see as much as possible of the people and countries," and "to show" in consequence that "the Crown is not merely an abstract symbol of our unity but a personal and living bond between you [the people of the Commonwealth] and me."

Such an excellent attitude to have - no taking the people for granted or neglecting to look them up and ask after them either.

Obviously, whenever and wherever she went to Commonwealth countries (where she was head of state in 14 of them), she put them and their Commonwealth on the world map *because her visits were globally televised*, and this was a very good thing for these nations, as well as being all part of her persistent presence as Britain's *Television Queen*, which is what this book is all about.

Ironically, she had been advised by her first Prime Minister, Winston Churchill (for whom she had the greatest respect and whose state funeral she attended) not to let television cameras into her wedding and royal affairs, but ignoring this advice was the best thing she ever did for putting herself and the Commonwealth on the map, as we shall see before we are through with this little book.

This well-intentioned advice from Churchill was ironic - history is full of ironies, is it not? - because it was precisely her royal *mystique* that was the very thing that actually prevented her from becoming globally and nationally popular.

Most people have had enough of centuries-old mystique and the deferment that went with it. They want their royals open and honest and transparent, so that they can hopefully understand them better, identify with and relate to them more clearly, engage with them and feel good about them, and it is this that the Queen of England cottoned onto fast.

This does not mean that they want their royals cycling around town and giving the V-sign to motorists, or queuing up in supermarkets necessarily - same as everybody else - but that they do want to know all about them in order to understand and value them better, to understand how their power is wielded and what their human-interest and other problems are; rather than being kept in the dark by intelligence-insulting and fairy-tale mystique.

They want their royals in-amongst them, not from Mars or The Other Side of the Moon!

And this is what they have got during the reign of the late Queen.

And most people all too clearly much prefer in the UK the national and tribal unity and dignity that their royals provide, with all the pageantry and ceremony that goes with it (such excellent theatre), they much prefer a dignified and stylish class-act to a mundane, tin-pot, shabby or mickey mouse royalty (too much mickey mouse is what they too often get from too many of their politicians!).

A united country - with unity and dignity of purpose, whether national or international - is what most Brits (millions of television viewers) vote for with their feet and get from their royals as they unreservedly turn out of them in their millions, preferring this to republicanism.

Whilst the most-travelled Queen in British history never visited Israel - presumably for political and security reasons - or Greece (presumably for distressing personal reasons relating to the
break-up and revolutionary overthrow of her husband Prince Philip's family and the break-up of its monarchy there) - she did reach out and travel to most other places, including Communist China (where she became the first royal to make a visit) and also Republican Eire (with its IRA forever bombing Britain and grinding its teeth!).

As a globe-trotting journalist all over East and West Europe (including Russia), North America (including Canada), Mexico, North and South Africa - as well as the Middle East, India, Hong Kong and Southeast Asia - I of course know from personal experience (all globe-trotters know or should know this, unless they have their heads where the sun doesn't shine!) that the natives in most countries generally prefer foreigners who are: not a mystery to them; are not aloof and unfriendly, as they stand on ceremony among them instead of greeting and meeting them warmly, treating them as equals and taking a genuine and caring interest in them (this is human nature, right?). They don't prefer foreigners who are insular and toffee nosed as they look down on them, or do not greet and meet them warmly and openly because they really are glad to see them (it is not rocket science to get one's head around this!).

And this is what the late Queen Elizabeth certainly knew and made a point of doing, greeting people openly and warmly, winning hearts and minds and influencing people for the better in this way worldwide, wherever she went.

All things considered, she did a good global and Commonwealth job that owed much to its being regularly televised and popularised by the cameras and having none of the long-standing mystique favoured by Winston Churchill who was of course a neo-Victorian during his time.

Whilst having no mystique is a double-edged sword - because it means that royals are clearly seen warts and all, with all their personal failings and feelings, as well as their virtues and strengths - it is a sword that the late Queen of England wielded well, on balance and for the most part for the better and the greater good, to very excellent effect, just as she set the tone and a good example in the Commonwealth to very good effect.

So long may it continue and here's to her, of course!

Chapter Two

The Queen that Went to the Moon

If you think the title of this chapter improbable, then you'd better read on, because it is a fascinating lesser-known fact about Queen Elizabeth II that she has, in fact, sent herself to the moon.

She has also been on the other side of the moon here on earth!

As already explained in the preface, I first wrote about British royals when I was *The Times* correspondent in Saudi Arabia in the 1970s where Queen Elizabeth was advised by the British ambassador in Jeddah to stay on her royal yacht during a state visit to the desert kingdom because of the Saudi's 'undignified handling of women.'

Saudi Arabia was, for sure, the other side of the moon here on earth for her and the rest of us in those distant times, more than thirty years ago.

However, the day was saved by getting Saudi royals onto the royal yacht instead of going on land to visit them. So all's well that ends well and it did end well because King Abdullah became the first Saudi King in 20 years to visit the UK where he was warmly received by Queen Elizabeth at Buckingham Palace in November 2007.

But the 1970s story about how Elizabeth boxed clever in the desert kingdom was one of the most important stories about British royals back then, because it revealed how Queen Elizabeth's state visits in some parts of the world are not always as easy as falling off a log, and it must surely be a memory that sticks in the mind as she looks back on her 60-year reign, unless, of course, she consciously dismisses it from her mind.

I have written a paperback book – *The Beheading and Other True Stories* (2011) - in which all the details of this are well documented and explained in chapter fourteen, for those interested to have chapter and verse on this subject. But I have not noticed that any of this year's Diamond Jubilee books that have been written about Elizabeth's reign thus far have mentioned this.

Most books about Queen Elizabeth II during her Diamond Jubilee year are, predictably, about her relationships with British prime ministers and/or about her role in the Commonwealth, two very well-worn and overdone subjects, about which we have already read much in the press previously.

But what else does Queen Elizabeth do for any other different kinds of books to be written about her?

Other than conduct relationships with prime ministers and commonwealth leaders, when not showing for her people at the grass roots in all sorts of ways, what else is new?

Probably there are some art books to be written about all the different portraits that she has sat for, and there are of course always the gossipy books about what royal and other insiders say about her and leak to the press, books about what royal correspondents in the press or on television say and think about her, not that their information is new either, given that it's all been said and done before.

But this *Television Queen* book is quite different and new because it falls into none of the existing categories, as it concentrates on only one aspect of her reign – that of her relationship with television, which seems to me to be the most important and most overlooked thing about her; overlooked by the millions who watch her on television without fully understanding the behind the scenes nature of her relationship with television, how it has come about, and how important it has been to her popularity and success.

Whilst prime ministers and commonwealth leaders come and go, British television and the British monarchy remain as permanent fixtures, with the latter needing to co-exist well with the former, because it is the former that presents her to her people and the world at large, not temporary prime ministers or commonwealth leaders.

If she does not get on with prime ministers, they will not openly criticise or expose her in the full glare of publicity, if they can help it.

But television and its news journalists certainly will at any time of the day or night, which is why she needs to make a success of her relationship with television – as indeed she has done - unlike her relationship with prime ministers, so many of whom have come and gone during her reign, as she has seen them all out.

The millions who watch her on television – for whom this book is chiefly but not exclusively written – are not the ones who read the books about how she does or does not get on with different prime ministers and/or commonwealth leaders and so remember her for this. Readers of these books run into tens of thousands, not millions.

But the millions are those who remember her from her television presence over the years, from her coronation to her Christmas Day speeches, the television programmes in which she has appeared, and how she has been reported and discussed on television.

This is what interests them most, not what the Queen's least favourite prime ministers thought about her and vice versa.

For these reasons, I have written this book in order to demonstrate that, more than anything else, Queen Elizabeth II is Britain's television queen and will be remembered for this in particular, by most people, in the fullness of time.

The affection that her admirers have for her comes mostly from television these days. They do not have to line the streets and flag-wave anymore, unless of course she is visiting their village or home town, and even then they can usually watch her on tele' (even so, many still turn out). But the majority who live far from the places that she visits, can still watch her, as if she were just down the road visiting their village or home town.

This is how television works its magic for her and how she, in turn, works her magic for television, in a mutually rewarding relationship – more viewers for television and more fans for her.

As already observed in the preface, Queen Elizabeth will of course be remembered for other things besides television, but it seems that the jewel in her crown in the 20th and 21st centuries has been television. And let us repeat that this is because she has existed for her people more powerfully and more visibly on their television screens than anywhere else and continues to do so to this day. Having gone out of her way to invite the television cameras into her life, at the expense of losing much if not most of her royal mystique, she has moved with the times and also ahead of the times where television has been concerned, demonstrating that she is indeed Britain's television queen.

As we shall see in these pages, there are arguably at least seven or eight convincing reasons for referring to Queen Elizabeth II as a television queen.

One can say that here is a monarch who is the inventor, metaphorically speaking, of televised coronations, whilst also being the most televised (and indeed visualised) royal in the world.

She is the first lady of reality-TV in Britain (which she also invented with Britain's first family reality-TV show) and, whilst reality-TV is not to everybody's taste, it is an historical fact that she invented it with supreme good taste once upon a time (not that much of it has any good taste anymore!).

In addition to all this, she has been the first royal friend and ally of television, the first and foremost TV celebrity with a TV fan club of millions who have repeatedly followed her on the box, including her aforesaid televised Christmas speeches, which is another of her inventions.

Here we have a significant number of 'firsts' for a once upon a time new monarch, in a relatively short space of time, when she became Queen of England.

Firsts that came in the following order:

1953 – First televised royal coronation in UK and World

1957 – First televised Queen's Speech on Christmas Day

1969 – First family reality-TV show in UK

1969 – First image of Queen Elizabeth sent to the moon!

Prior to 1953 she made her first (but not the first) Christmas Day radio speech in 1952 after her father died, continuing a radio tradition that began in 1932, and then she upgraded to television in 1953 from Sandringham House in Norfolk where it was filmed for television.

The above sequence of events contrasts with the invention of television in the UK as follows:

1925 – The world's first moving TV images in London

1929 – The first BBC television broadcast in London

1936 – The world's first public service TV launched in UK

1939 – World War Two Prevents Further Progress!

Whilst these first television moving TV-images were the invention of John Logie Baird in England, he was not the sole inventor of television, as we shall see in chapter four.

But it is against this background that Queen Elizabeth II has become Britain's television queen, thanks in no small part to the pioneering ingenuity and invention of those of her loyal subjects who were mostly physicists, electronic and television engineers long before she came to her throne.

Last Christmas, her Christmas Day speech came fifth, after *East Enders* in first place for the highest viewing figures on Christmas Day.

Fifth may not sound very impressive, but with more than eight million viewers, it puts her comfortably in the top ten most-watched TV programmes, which is where she needs to be, if she is to have a fan base that enables British monarchy to survive in the 21st century (as she and her Buckingham Palace advisors understand only too well).

Whilst she was some 4 million viewers behind *East Enders*, so too were other television programmes behind her.

Finally - in the seven or eight reasons why Queen Elizabeth II can be accurately referred to as Britain's television queen – comes the convincing reason that her kingdom (or queendom) is the world's home of television (as we have seen in the foregoing).

Her kingdom is where the science and technologies were invented for the first public service TV in the world, setting the stage for when she originally came along in the early 1950s, during Britain's most significant television decade that launched her into the global television age in which we all live today.

We have here the key - albeit lesser-known - reasons why she became Britain's television queen, even though few of these reasons are generally understood by most people in Britain and the world at large.

If you doubt that this is not generally understood, try asking your friends and colleagues if they think that Queen Elizabeth II is Britain's television queen and, if so, why and for how many significant reasons?

See how many reasons they can give you.

Of course academic historians will be the final judge – and this little book is simply a popular history for the masses, the first draft perhaps of Queen Elizabeth II's television history – but it would seem that her television role is what the queen will and should be remembered for most of all, which is why I have written about this in order to make my case, as a possible contribution to royal history, television scientific and media history, and to intellectual thought on this matter.

As we can see from all this, television fell into her lap and she had the good sense to make the most and the best of it.

More recently we have seen the following television programmes about her and her family:

1992: *Queen Elizabeth R*, a BBC-TV documentary.

2006: Rolph Harris painting Queen Elizabeth on TV.

2007: *Monarchy: The Royal Family at Work* by the BBC.

When Elizabeth agreed to be televised with the Australian pop-artist, Rolph Harris, as shown above in 2006 - while he painted a quick and sketchy portrait of her - she engaged in some harmless and skimpy chat about royal art-portraits, but nothing more than that, and she was quite crisp and monosyllabic in the small talk that she had with him.

So this was very far from being a proper TV interview.

Even so, it was the first time that the nation saw her in some kind of conversation with a mere mortal while being painted by him. It was not unlike a not very sociable woman chatting with her hairdresser and keeping it brief and to the point. But it was, for all that, a continuing part of Queen Elizabeth outing herself on television, coming out and showing for her people.

By the same token, on her 2011 state visit to Eire – another first for her after all the many long and protracted troubles with the Irish – she showed for the television talent show *X Factor* by agreeing to meet the Irish *X Factor* singer and supermarket worker, Mary Byrne, telling her that she liked the show.

X Factor is not a pure talent show because it also features very mediocre amateur entertainers with no talent whatsoever – who would not have been allowed to show their face in earlier times - and it would seem from this that the millions who watch it are good humoured enough to watch the talentless along with the talented (and this must include Queen Elizabeth if, as she told Mary Byrne, she really does enjoy the show).

Making entertainment out of a glaring absence of talent is part of the show's agenda, but the *X* in the show's title stands for *extra*, for the discovery of talented singers and other entertainers with something extra, some of whom are very good indeed and able to demonstrate that they do, indeed, have the *X-factor*.

But, sadly, they are few and far between these days, so viewers are having to put up with a lot of dross besides, otherwise there would be no show, and no discovery of the little new and deserving talent that there is.

By showing for *X Factor*, Britain's television queen was doing what she does best, popularising herself with millions of viewers and promoting her image thereby, turning television viewers into her fans, maybe, staying close to and reaching out to her people – doing whatever it takes to remain popular.

When she did this in 2007 for BBC's *Monarchy: The Royal Family at Work* (also known as *A Year With the Queen*), things went badly wrong with this, her second reality-TV fly on the wall programme, following on from the first one in 1969, with which she was said to be disappointed because she thought that it made her and her family look too ordinary (as we shall see in chapter five).

Things went wrong in 2007 when a film clip was shown of Queen Elizabeth supposedly storming out of a photographic session with the American photographer from New York, Annie Leibowitz, when in truth Elizabeth was doing no such thing.

On the contrary she was storming in!

Yet BBC producer, Peter Fincham, told journalists that Elizabeth had indignantly walked out because Annie had asked her to remove her crown. He reportedly said that Elizabeth was seen 'losing it a bit and walking out in a huff.'

Because the BBC had, in fact, breached its contract with Buckingham Palace in this way, the matter was put into the hands of the law firm, Farrer & Co, as a result of which the BBC formally apologised to Queen Elizabeth, leaving its producer to resign.

It was Farrer & Co, traditional lawyers to the British monarchy, that represented Paul McCartney in his divorce settlement with his former (second) wife Heather Mills and I wrote about this in *The Times* newspaper on May 6th 2008 when Heather Mills chucked a glass of water over the head of Paul's QC, Fiona Shackleton, otherwise known as 'the steel magnolia.'

So it's not only on television that things can go wrong!

But in the law courts also.

Paul McCartney wrote a pop song for Queen Elizabeth entitled *Her Majesty* that featured in a Beatles' Abbey Road album in 1969 and it was played again at the *Party at the Palace* in 2002 for the occasion of Queen Elizabeth's Golden Jubilee.

But, as we see from the *Royal Family at Work* reality-TV show, there are of course risks involved when royals go public and get themselves televised on fly-on-the-wall programmes of this sort, which is why television is such a double-edged sword that cuts both ways, and can work against a good image projection for royals, as well as well for it. Television cuts both ways, not that this had ever deterred Britain's television queen.

On balance, the results of Queen Elizabeth's television activities have been more in her favour than against her, and these major recent developments in her television history (since the 1950s and 1960s) have continued to keep her in the public eye, as planned.

In the meantime, there have been television programmes featuring other members of her family, as well as the usual run of the mill news coverage for her, not to mention the annual televised *Remembrance Day* ceremonies that come and go every year.

In terms of viewing figures, all this coverage stacks up handsomely for British royalty and also for British television that would not be the same without royalty.

So all things considered, Queen Elizabeth has been a massively televised monarch throughout her reign, the first of her kind in British history, which is why of course she is Britain's television queen.

Whilst she has not, as yet, been personally interviewed on television, she has in all other respects been very active and pioneering, trying out new sorts of programmes.

BBC Radio Four presenter, John Humphrys has openly declared that it is his ambition to interview her and it remains to be seen whether she will be interviewed either on radio or television, but she tends to leave the big television interviews to her son and heir, Prince Charles, who is not camera shy where television interviews are concerned, but that's another story.

Given that we are currently in the celebratory 2012 Diamond Jubilee Year of Queen Elizabeth II, now is the time to reflect upon all these things about her and her 60-year reign, and the shared times in which we and she live, to reflect on what we make of these times and how we rate her.

But if we rate her as a television queen, how else do we/should we rate her?

What else is there and how does it compare with her activities on television?

And how can we rate her as a television queen without also rating the scientific history of television, which is no less interesting than the history of the House of Windsor, as I imagine most royals and fans of royalty must surely agree.

Regardless of whether we are royalists or republicans, this is the year for considering exactly what kind of monarch Queen Elizabeth II has been and the way in which her image has become truly televised and truly global.

But the Queen's televised (and filmed) image is not only global. It has also visited outer space, would you believe?

As we have seen in this chapter already, this was in 1969 - the year in which she was also making, Britain's first family-reality TV show - when she sent a micro-filmed message on July 21st to accompany the first moon landing of the Apollo II astronauts from the United States, telling them that 'on behalf of the British people, I salute the skill and courage which have brought man to the moon. May this endeavour increase the knowledge and well-being of mankind.'

Not many people know that.

They do not know that, when man first went to the moon and landed there, the Queen of England went with him!

If Queen Elizabeth II and television/film are not made for each other, it is hard to know what is; and whilst they have not always been natural running mates, they have nevertheless been natural for enough of the time for her to become a fully-fledged television queen, who has wisely understood the value of trading her royal mystique in return for television exposure and celebrity.

Whilst traditional royalists may wish that our royals had more privacy and mystique, they need to recognise that the British monarch cannot have it both ways. Regular television exposure, without losing much of her mystique in the process, is not an option.

The loss of mystique is the price that royalty has to pay these days if it intends to survive, as Queen Elizabeth certainly intends that it will survive.

Given that she is the monarch who has put royalty on the television map, one can only assume that she knows what she is doing and exactly what she is up against, and is on the whole well pleased with the outcome, as most of her people certainly are.

She and they are well pleased because she is reckoned to have some 80% approval-rating from them in the MORI public opinion polls (July 2006, Mori Trends) – and where does most of the public get its opinions from if not chiefly from watching her on television where it arrives at its opinions?

But an approval rating does not mean that most people are necessarily in favour of monarchy in preference to a republic. This is because the pollsters' questions for approval are usually, along the lines - do you approve of Queen Elizabeth *as a queen, as queens go, do you think she is a good queen*? Implying do you approve of her demeanour, personality and conduct etc, to which an impressive 80% have reportedly said yes.

But this is not the same as asking if they prefer monarchy to republicanism?

However, even when this question is asked, the pollsters tell that more than 50% of the population have said yes.

So with more than 50% of the people in favour of monarchy and another 80% approving Queen Elizabeth at the last count in 2006, she is quite clearly on a roll, she who invented herself as Britain's television queen, beginning with the invention of televised coronations and also televised royalty, as we shall see in the following chapter.

Chapter Three

Inventing Televised Royalty

As we see already, there is quite a lot that most people do not know about Queen Elizabeth II and her reign, but there's more yet, much more.

Not only did she invent televised royalty for the first time, at her coronation back in 1953, but she also invented Britain's first fly-on-the-wall royal reality-TV programme, in addition to Britain's first live television Christmas speech by a monarch.

There are those who think that it made more sense to do the televised speeches, than a reality-TV programme, and the word is that she was disappointed with the outcome of her 1969 reality-TV programme, because it made her too ordinary and maybe even gimmicky (did Princess Anne really read a book at the breakfast table?). But whatever the outcome, this programme shows what a television queen she had become by the late 1960s, and how she was prepared to experiment.

She furthermore invented a new life for British monarchy in the 21st century on You Tube, Facebook, Podcast and Twitter and became the first British monarch to send an email and have her own private email address.

So, in addition to all else for which she is being celebrated this year, she should certainly be celebrated for having been Britain's first television, social media and mass communications queen.

But television is what started it all and remains the jewel in her crown (so, too, did her interested in photography, perhaps, given that it is listed as one of her chief interests, together with horse riding and racing, and her dogs).

Queen Elizabeth's coronation – when she was 25 years of age – was in 1953, a year after she succeeded her father who died in his sleep in 1952, and the reason why her coronation came twelve months later was because that is how long it took to plan and organise it, as well as to plan the televising of the event that the British government and establishment did not want on the nation's and the world's television screens.

Queen Elizabeth's father was King George V1, recently featured in the fictionalised 2010 Oscar-winning film, *The King's Speech*, an historical drama for which Colin Firth won a best actor award for playing King George who was the king with a mighty stutter who turned to a speech therapist to help him overcome his speech defect, after his impromptu and unexpected ascension to the British throne.

This was when his brother King Edward, the Duke of Windsor, suddenly abdicated in order to marry Wallis Simpson, an American commoner and divorcee, treated by British royalty and the establishment as if she were a scarlet woman destined to be a leper, not just because she was common, but also because she was a divorcee. *The Kings Speech* film won four Oscars, including one for Helena Bonham Carter who played a young Queen Mother (Queen Elizabeth II's late mother).

King George V1 was an acute smoker who died of lung cancer and his dead body was found in his bed by a servant at Sandringham where the king had also been born 56 years previously – found whilst his daughter and heir apparent, Princess Elizabeth, was holidaying in Kenya in a hunting lodge with her husband, the Duke of Edinburgh whom she had married in 1947, six years before her coronation.

In 1953 when Queen Elizabeth II was crowned at a magnificent coronation ceremony in Westminster Abbey in front of 8,000 VIP guests – including high and mighty heads of state and foreign royals from all over the world as well as ministers in the British government – an estimated 20 million people watched the ceremony on television in Britain and throughout the world, and it was the first time that a British or any other coronation had ever been televised in the centuries-long history of monarchy.

This was a turning point in history, not only for television, but for the affairs of state and the conduct of British monarchy – the televised conduct of monarchy.

Whilst the time for television had come, there were still those who were telling her to avoid it like the plague!

But it was entirely due to the daring of the young 25-year-old Elizabeth – who has now reached the ripe old age of 86 years (her husband Prince Philip, the Duke of Edinburgh, is four years her senior) - that millions were able to watch the event back then.

It was due to her because, when she was advised by the old guard, including the then Prime Minister Winston Churchill and his government, to resist the intrusive television cameras and not allow them into the Abbey, she ignored their advice.

They argued that, to let the cameras in, would be the beginning of the end of the mystique of British royalty, and so it was.

But the end of royal mystique was, in many ways, the making of royalty in latter-day Britain and the world, where television has won and kept many more fans for British royalty as a result of its new-found transparency.

But, lock the cameras out at all costs, is what Queen Elizabeth II's advisors suggested to her at the outset of her reign.

However, she would not listen, so the televising of her coronation went ahead without her government's approval, because she took matters into her own hands, and in this way she became, using her own initiative, Britain's television queen in the days when monarchs had not previously had much time for television, which had existed for 17 years in Britain as a public service since 1936, the first public service in the world.

Various programmes had been transmitted from Alexander Palace – or 'Ally Pally,' as it was nicknamed by the Lancashire factory-girl pop singer, Gracie Fields, in those days, a nickname that remains to this day (my maternal grandfather was a close friend of Gracie Fields, but that's another story).

It was a sign of the times that television was beginning to be taken seriously in Britain when Queen Elizabeth II came to her throne, after it had not been taken seriously previously, when it had been happily regarded by the establishment as a bit of a joke, which is how they wanted it to remain. They wanted this so that it would keep its nose out of the affairs of state that were conducted by an elite and exclusive upper-class few who ran the country without close scrutiny and wanted things to continue that way.

They did not want television meddling in their affairs, in a country deeply divided by class, divided in their favour.

But Queen Elizabeth II was much more forward-thinking and open-minded and she alone did take television seriously and was more prepared to give this menacing thing called television the benefit of the doubt.

Previous television programmes, with poor image-definition, had included variety entertainments, the occasional documentary, news, cartoons, big band and sports programmes, as well as a largely failed attempt at televising the coronation *procession* – not the coronation - of Queen Elizabeth II's father, George VI in 1937, a decade and a half previously.

This procession was *outside*, not inside Westminster Abbey in amongst the great and the good, and only the procession, not the entire coronation ceremony, was to be televised.

But picture transmissions got embarrassingly lost, due to faulty equipment and/or cameras and transmissions, and viewers reported that they did and/or did not receive occasional images in different parts of the country!

Thankfully, this event in 1937 was also filmed, so it was shown in cinemas.

Initially, Alexander Palace transmissions were generally not capable of reaching beyond a 40 mile radius from Muswell Hill in North London, however there were sometimes reports of images being picked up beyond that radius, but not without difficulty.

The last TV news report, before television was taken off air prior to the outbreak of World War Two with Germany in 1939, was by Richard Dimbleby from Heston Airport when prime minister Neville Chamberlain famously returned from Munich in 1938, with his 'peace in our time,' piece of paper signed by Hitler, which proved, as we know, not to be worth the paper it was written on. Heston Airport, in the days before London Heathrow, was in Hounslow to the West of London (as of course is Heathrow today).

When Britain went to war with Germany there were an estimated 19,000 electronic television sets in the UK, as opposed to 1,600 in Germany and 7/8,000 in the United States.

So there can be no doubt that Britain was in a lead position. It was the home of television where it had first been invented and run as a public service for the benefit of the people.

There was also a patent for three-dimensional imagery that had been taken out in Britain as early as the 1890s by the British film director, William Friesse Green, for a 3-D movie device.

122 years later, in China today, a new 3-D television channel is currently being introduced for the first time in that country, and in the 1950s when Queen Elizabeth II was getting into her stride as the new Queen, 3-D movies were appearing in cinemas, chiefly in the United States, although 3-D television with electromechanical cathode-ray tubes existed in Britain in the late 1920s and early 1930s.

But it was not until after World War Two that television improved massively and suddenly became a force to be reckoned with, the suddenness of which was too much for British governments and the establishment that sill did not want the new medium to be taken seriously.

But this was not too sudden for the young Queen Elizabeth II who was light years ahead of her government and other royals in this respect.

But the prophesy of the old guard that she and her family would lose their mystique if she embraced the cameras, has of course proved to be correct, not that there was anything that a young new Queen could sensibly have done to have prevented such an immovable force as television, other than plunge her head deep into the sand with the other ostriches around her, which she declined to do.

She was *not* an ostrich queen.

Whilst today's staunch royalists may prefer monarchy to hang on to what is left of its mystique, there are many others in the 21st century who think that monarchy is the better for not having any mystique, and that old-style mystique is no longer remotely possible or even desirable in the modern world. They take the view that if monarchy is to survive it has to be without mystique these days, because in previous generations mystique had veiled a multitude of sins.

Even allowing for all the embarrassing royal scandals that finish up on TV, many of these scandals make the royals look more human and more like their subjects where sexual, domestic and marital matters are concerned.

For these reasons it is arguable that monarchy has become like television soap opera with brass knobs on and everybody, it seems, is perfectly happy with this, including monarchy by and large and most of the time, because it still keeps its doors open to television, as it always has since Elizabeth arrived on the scene.

From the outset of her reign, one could see that Queen Elizabeth II was a new queen with her head screwed on and with a mind of her own with regard to television, not that too many people realise this today, and certainly not her critics, and not that royal correspondents in the media often if at all ever talk of this (when researching and sifting through history, different things grab the imagination of some observers but not others).

The British establishment and its governments in the early days of television believed that a public television service was all very well, but not if it included or attempted to include royalty, which had hitherto been treated as an ivory-tower institution until Queen Elizabeth II came along.

It was only after protracted discussions and arguments about whether or not to televise her coronation that Elizabeth ran out of patience and overruled the British government, saying that it was she who was being crowned, not her cabinet ministers!

Whilst she was non-political and could not interfere with her government's politics, her coronation was her own affair, not theirs.

This is well documented in *The Year That Made the Day*, published by the BBC, and right throughout this year of preparations that went into organising the 1953 coronation, the BBC was well aware that televising the event might be called off at any moment!

But, as things turned out, Queen Elizabeth II was on the side of the corporation and of television.

Because televising this event – with Geoffrey Fisher the Archbishop of Canterbury putting the crown on Elizabeth's head - was indeed the beginning of the end of royal mystique, one might have expected a new monarch to get cold feet, however she was a new and futuristic monarch who was undeterred.

She would hear nothing of turning her back on television, or turning back the clock for that matter. On the contrary she would let the cameras in, rather than keeping them out, and she would not allow her monarchy to be stuck in the dark ages of an un-televised past, and good for her (as we have seen, her father's coronation had been filmed in local cinemas on newsreels, not televised, as it ought to have been).

Her decision to let her coronation be televised resulted in the public demand for television sets doubling in the UK where the number of licences doubled to 3 million. Clearly, her coronation was good for television business, and no doubt the new Queen hoped that television would be good for the business of royalty also.

She could see that it would have been suicidal for British monarchy to have turned its back on television and the British people thereby, and she was quick to realise this when others were not. On the question of her loss of mystique, she was damned if she did go along with television and damned if she did not, but for all that, she decided to grasp the nettle and give television a try.

The thing to remember about her and her family and its various members is that they are very much a technological family. They are not arty or literary, or scholastic or intellectual, creative or overly cultured types. From the Duke of Edinburgh and the Queen to their children and grand children, they variously fly aeroplanes and helicopters and command ships at sea, using a practical can-do intelligence and expertise to that end, when they are not otherwise riding horses and serving in the military with undoubted courage and practical military skills and expertise, putting their lives on the line for their country, like everybody else, or otherwise hunting, shooting and fishing.

But they are not bookish or literary, and certainly not philosophical or intellectual thinkers, but practical and sporty rather, and interested in technology and engineering. This applies not least the Duke of Edinburgh with his high-command naval career, and to the Queen who, during World War II, was given an honorary commission in the volunteer Women's Auxiliary Territorial Service (ATS) that was formed in 1938 as a branch of the British Army. In the ATS she trained as a mechanic as well as a driver. It was not nursing or medicine that interested her, but mechanics and fixing things.

Having been educated by private tutors at home, Queen Elizabeth did not have a broad-based education as a child – reportedly she had only done a bit of royal and constitutional history, some reading, writing and some foreign languages, and perhaps a little music – but there is no suggestion that she did any maths or sciences, biology, geography, art and so on. Nor, it seems, did she study for more than half a day.

What we are told is that she was a well-behaved, disciplined, orderly and responsible little girl who grew up to love dogs, horses and the English countryside, and that she also grew up to be practical enough to train as a mechanic and driver in the ATS.

But having married a very practical royal navy officer, with a good grasp of science and technology, no doubt her children and family became technological, as it were, as a result of his influence.

No doubt Elizabeth increasingly realised the importance of technology and science in this way, not least at sea (we can only surmise and logically deduce this, given that not much information of Queen Elizabeth's educational abilities is generally available).

It is precisely because Philip's special interests are chiefly in scientific and technological research and development – aside from sport, the welfare of young people, conservation and the environment – that there is very little about British industrial and scientific life with which he is not familiar, and he has been a regular visitor to research stations and laboratories with the aim of, he says, understanding British industrial life better and helping to contribute to its improvement if he possibly can.

He is a former President of the British Association for the Advancement of Sciences, back in 1952, and he serves or has served as Chancellor of the universities of Cambridge, Edinburgh, Salford and Wales, in addition to being a Life Governor of King's College, London, and

Patron of the London Guildhall University. He is also Grand Master of the Guild of Air Pilots and Air Navigators.

In view of all the Duke's scientific and technological interests – even before he married Queen Elizabeth as well as the early years thereafter (and subsequently throughout her reign) – it would be surprising indeed if he had not brought up a technological family of his own and if he had not imparted his knowledge to his wife and his children.

So, when television came along, it was perhaps even less that Queen Elizabeth was interested at least in the scientific and technological breakthrough and wonders of television.

As for its cultural, social and political implications, that was another matter, but for sure here was a queen that was not likely to turn her back on television unless she positively had to, even if television did turn out to be easier said than done for her in the fullness of time where protecting her family's privacy and her royal image and mystique was concerned.

Here was a queen with an eye for the opportunity of television, even though it was a double-edged sword.

But television was not just a double-edged sword for her, but for Geoffrey Fisher, the Archbishop of Canterbury likewise, he who put the crown on the new Queen's head. It was a double-edged sword for him because he was widely publicised and criticised for having stated that, for all he knew, it was 'within the providence of God that the human race should destroy itself' in a nuclear war (against the Soviet Union).

So if God willed the end of the world in this way, then there was no point resisting or preventing it, or doing anything about it, let alone winning it!

This was the unenlightened religious and political climate in 1953 when Queen Elizabeth II started her reign.

Television had been jump-started by electromagnetism that had existed in Britain as early as 1831 in the days of the English inventor, the Londoner Michael Faraday, the acknowledged father of global electricity and electrical generation.

Whilst photo conductivity and image transmissions of one kind or another had been well underway in Britain, Europe (the cathode-ray tube had been invented in Germany) and North America, including the scanning and faxing of images, engineers and inventors in several countries – Britain, France, Germany, Russia, Canada and the United States - had all been exploring the possibility of television and experimenting to that end.

The necessary electromechanical methods of scanning and of photography, and the transmission and reproduction of images, as well as the development of display tubes - en-route to all-electronic broadcast television - was well underway internationally, and sooner or later one of the competing countries would make a breakthrough and get to the finishing line ahead of the others, as Britain did in a very close-run race.

But had the British not got to the finishing line first, others would have done so in quick succession, given that developments in television were in full swing in the developed countries.

There was a kind of space race underway between nations to become the first to fill the space on the world's television screens, and it soon became clear that, whoever did it first, would soon be overtaken by the United States for perfectly obvious politico-economic and financial investment reasons. The Americans had deeper pockets and bigger markets in every respect.

The reason why the BBC dropped the British television inventor, John Logie Baird – who, as already observed, was not the sole inventor of television - in favour of America's Marconi in 1937, was because quality of image reproduction with Marconi was said to be twice as good as Baird's.

The inventors of television had been all those who had previously invented the physics (Sir Isaac Newton), the electricity and its generators, the cathode-ray tube, the disk-scanning and the photography.

It had been a gas-lit Buckingham Palace that had been installed with electricity for the first time – in its glittering ballroom – in 1883 in the days of Queen Victoria, but it was a fully switched on and all-electric palace when Elizabeth II's parents and their children came along.

So the scene was set for all things electric, including television before long.

In the year 1900 the Russian Constantine Persky had first coined the word 'television' in a lecture that he delivered at the World's Trade Fair in Paris. So there really was nothing new about television when the doors were opened at Westminster Abbey to let in the cameras in 1953.

What was new was a future Queen coming out in favour of televising her coronation and raising a goodly number of eye brows in government and palace circles, no doubt irritating some of her closest advisors.

Of mixed Greek and Latin origin – *tele* from the Ancient Greek and *visio* from Latin – the word television means 'far sighted' and it was the young Queen of England who had been far sighted enough to see that television was to be the future, and not least for royalty, after the British had also been far sighted enough as a nation to get the show on the road at Alexander Palace in 1936.

But whilst television was not invented by any one person – as we have seen, there were Germans, French, Russians and Americans all with a finger in the pie - it was a Scottish inventor living and working in England, the aforesaid John Loggie Baird, who gave the first public demonstration of televised silhouette-images in motion at Selfridges Department Store in the heart of the West End shopping district of London in 1926, followed by a second demonstration at London's Royal Institution in 1927.

That a scientific institution had to take a lead from a department store speaks volumes for establishmentarian attitudes back then.

Whilst Logie Baird had developed the disk-scanning equipment to make television possible, the world's aforementioned first commercially applicable cathode-ray tube had been invented by a German called Ferdinand Braun, but Baird was the one who first came up with the images and, when he first demonstrated them to amazed shopper in Selfridges, they were invited to buy his variously priced television sets for anything from £20 to £150, and to receive them as and when they became available. Meanwhile, in the United States, an American called Filo Farnsworth had been busily putting together a television set of his own, for which he first applied for a patent in 1927.

But even before Braun and Baird there had been an Englishman as early as 1878 who had invented a cathode-ray tube that was not commercially ready – when the world and its markets were not ready for it – and that was Sir William Crookes without whose first tube the later tubes would have certainly have been seriously delayed before they came on stream.

Crooke's motto was 'love one another, educate yourselves' (as he had done).

He was a Londoner, born in 1832, the eldest son of a tailor of North Country origin, and he married a girl from Darlington in Yorkshire.

Grammar school, but not university educated, Crookes was taken on as an assistant at the Royal College of Chemistry in London's Hanover Square, where he received his higher education.

Leaving the college later on, he became Superintendent of the Meteorological Department of the Radcliffe Observatory in Oxford, before going on to Chester Training College in the North Country as a chemistry lecturer.

Returning to London thereafter as a science journalist, consultant, lecturer, government adviser and inventor, he founded *Chemical News*, making enough money to live in the fashionable Kensington Park Gardens where he carried out his experiments in his private laboratory in the applied sciences. He became president of the Chemical Society, the Institution of Electrical Engineers and the Royal Society, getting himself knighted into the bargain.

Having discovered thallium in 1861, he went on to discover the phenomenon of the cathode-ray tube, having demonstrated the all-important understanding that cathode rays consisted of charged particles and not of electromagnetic radiation.

Cathode rays are a stream of electrons emitted by a cathode when voltage is applied between a cathode and an anode, either in a glass tube, or a tube containing low-pressure gas. It is these rays that are used in radar screens, oscilloscopes and the television tubes in television receivers.

Obviously, without this vital element, there could be no invention of television. The tube itself is a vacuum that converts electrical signals into visible forms by projecting a beam of electrons onto a fluorescent screen, which is why it is an absolutely essential component of a television receiver. Without it there can be no reception, no images on the screen, not television.

Clearly, Crookes was on to a winner.

He had made a tremendously important breakthrough, one of the greatest discoveries of all anywhere in the world.

Thanks to him and his discovery it was now possible to invent television.

No wonder he received honorary doctorates in science from Oxford and Cambridge universities, as well as from Sheffield and Durham universities, and academic awards, distinctions and medals from academies in Paris, Rome, Berlin, Washington, Philadelphia, Stockholm and Rotterdam and Cape Town.

No wonder he was knighted by the British government.

His discovery was 19 years ahead of the German cathode-ray tube that was discovered by the physicist Karl Braun, and some 48 years ahead of the invention of television in England and the Untied States.

As men of science go, William Crookes was a titan, yet who has heard of him today, or thinks of him when they talk of the invention of television?

Almost certainly, Queen Elizabeth II and other members of the British royal family will not have been overly or at all aware of him when, in 1953, they and the British government were debating whether or not to allow the Queen's coronation to be televised!

Few people today realise the television background to Queen Elizabeth II and her reign, either because they are not old enough to remember it, or have not read about it, or if they are old enough, then because most of them have forgotten it in the passage of time – 59/60 years - between 1952/3 and 2012.

Few people these days are aware of the truly amazing centuries-old tradition of the English in discovering and inventing computers, electricity, the internet, and so many other things besides. Few Brits understand this these days because this is a history that is no longer taught in schools.

The only reason that I know about it is partly because I have made it my business to find out and partly because my father – another self-educated inventor of sorts – filled my head with these stories, which I later checked out for myself.

When Queen Elizabeth II came to her throne, my family was only able to watch her coronation on television because my father generated his own electricity in the back garden of our 1950s gas-lit house in Reading, 40 miles West of London in Berkshire, the first and only working-class house to have electricity in the entire town.

I include mention of this in these pages because it is a reminder of how Queen Elizabeth's nation was for the majority of people at that time, most of whom were without television unless, like my father, they could generate it for themselves, which most could not.

In the absence of mains electricity services, many people still lived in gas-lit houses and those that did not, in certain parts of the country, certainly could not afford to buy a television set.

My father bought all his generating and other equipment from World War Two army surplus stores and installed it in a suitably silenced brick-built shed that he constructed especially for the purpose in our back garden, as a result of which – hey presto! – we suddenly had television and electricity throughout the house when our neighbours did not.

We also had a radio that he put together himself and a cinematograph, the hired celluloid films of which – in big circular cans – he projected onto the walls (to begin with) of our house until he could afford to get in some screens that he could hang on the walls instead. He turned the handle of the cinematograph machine so that we could all watch silent movies in our home.

But on one occasion, something went wrong with our back garden electricity generator that exploded in consequence, blowing the roof off the shed, some five or ten minutes after he had left it (so a lucky escape for him!), and also sending our cat, that was reclined on the roof, flying through the air (but it landed on its feet, so another lucky escape!).

The generator went up in flames, while my parents and I and my elder brother rushed into the garden with buckets of tap water from the scullery (called kitchen today) to put out the flames, as the neighbours looked on in utter astonishment.

My father had previously built his own racing car – in the days before motor cars for the masses – the brakes of which failed on another occasion when he collided with the chauffeur-driven Rolls Royce of the chairman of Huntley & Palmers biscuit factory in Reading!

In those distant days most householders did everything for themselves, fixing everything – including the plumbing etc and chimney-sweeping in coal-fired, gas-lit houses – and they took pride in being able to do everything for themselves.

As we see, this really is an eye-opener to the kind of nation and the kind of subjects with which Queen Elizabeth II found herself in pos-war Britain, prior to the arrival of the 1960s, when everything changed very much for the better for ordinary people.

Had my father been born in the 1950s or 1960s or later on in the 20th century – instead of leaving school at 12 years of age in the early part of the 20th century – he would have been an electronics or automobile engineer, but that's another story.

But the point is that our family would not have been able to watch Queen Elizabeth II's coronation had he not used his initiative and intelligence to generate his own electricity ahead of the local council and its electricity providers who were only serving the upper and middle-class parts of the town, not the working-class parts.

Today there is an awful lot that people do not know about Britain and the way that it was in its recent history when Queen Elizabeth came to her throne in 1952 and was crowned in 1953.

The royal family has diarised its involvement with the latest 20th and 21st century developments in technology as follows:

1878 – Queen Victoria met Alexander Graham Bell to try out his newly invented telephone ('a professor Bell explained the whole process which is most extraordinary,' the queen wrote in her diary).

1918: The first ever mass communication from a reigning British monarch was sent out in the form of a lithographed letter from George V, copied to all returning prisoners of war ('the queen joins me in welcoming you on your release from the miseries and hardships, which you have endured with so much patience and courage').

1932: King George V made his first Christmas Broadcast on radio ('I speak now from my home and from my heart to you all; to men and women so cut off by the snows, the desert, or the sea, that only voices out of air can reach them').

1937: The coronation *procession* of George VI became the first *outside* TV broadcast. This was only an outside procession going inside Westminster Abbey, not a full coronation service.

1940: Princess Elizabeth (the future Queen Elizabeth II) made her first-ever radio broadcast, accompanied by her sister Princess Margaret, on BBC's Children's Hour ('I feel that I am speaking to friends and companions who have shared with my sister and myself many happy children's hours').

1947: Princess Elizabeth made another radio broadcast to Britain's commonwealth countries on the occasion of her 21st birthday from South Africa ('I declare before you all that my whole life whether it be long or short shall be devoted to your service').

1953: Queen Elizabeth II allowed television cameras *inside* Westminster Abbey for the first time during a state occasion to televise her coronation, thereby inventing televised coronations for the first time (against the advice of her government).

1957: Queen Elizabeth II gave the first live Christmas broadcast on television ('that it is possible for some of you to see me today is just another example of the speed at which things are changing all around us…..television has made it possible for many of you to see me in your homes,' which her government had previously tried to prevent)

1958: Queen Elizabeth II made the first telephone trunk-call from Bristol to Edinburgh.

1969: Queen Elizabeth II sent a micro-filmed message to the moon to accompany the first landing there by the Apollo II astronauts from the USA. Her message read: 'On behalf of the British people, I salute the skill and courage which have brought man to the moon. May this endeavour increase the knowledge and well-being of mankind.'

1976: Queen Elizabeth II became the first British monarch to send an email! During a visit to an army base.

1977: Queen Elizabeth II launched www.royal.gov.uk during a visit to Kingsbury High School in Brent.

2002: 3,521 journalists from over 60 countries were accredited via an internet-based virtual press office to cover the events marking the Queen's Golden Jubilee.

2006: Queen Elizabeth II's Christmas Broadcast, otherwise known as The Queen's Speech, went on podcast for the fist time.

2007: Queen Elizabeth II launched the first Royal Channel on You Tube.

2008: Queen Elizabeth II uploaded a video to You Tube during a visit to Google's London office.

2009: A new versions of www.royal.gov.uk was launched by Queen Elizabeth II

2009: A British Monarchy Twitter account was launched at www.twitter.com/British Monarchy.

2010: Queen Elizabeth II visited Research in Motion (RIM) headquarters in Toronto during a visit to Canada.

2010: A British Monarchy Flickr account was launched.

2010: A British Monarchy Facebook account was launched.

As we see from the above, Queen Elizabeth II is no stranger to television, media and mass communications technology, in so many of the key developments of which she has been involved in one way or another, as suggested to her and arranged for her by others with the necessary expertise.

She is Britain's first and most technologically aware monarch.

She has followed her father's 'voices out of air' with her own 'images out of air.'

Because all doors have been open to her, she has become, without doubt, Britain's television queen, you-tube queen, face-book queen, twitter queen, podcast queen, giving away her mystique in all these areas, in order to move with the times.

She has been the first British and any other monarch to embrace all these technological developments, rather than turning her back on them, in order to reach out to her fans in every conceivable way. The public relations and marketing potential of mass communications in the modern world has by no means been lost on her. On the contrary she has moved with the times big time.

Because we live in a television age, we all take it for granted that everything washes up on the great sea shore of television, absolutely everything, including royalty, and we cannot imagine a life without television, or television without British royalty.

But, as we have seen, it was not forever thus and, when Queen Elizabeth II first came to her throne, the television age was only just seriously beginning as an increasingly commercial and popular public service, and it was by no means taken for granted that a royal coronation would of course have to be televised. On the contrary, the Queen's coronation was very nearly not televised. All she had to do was to say the word and it would not have been on people's television screens.

Her coronation would have been reserved for the eyes of a privileged few inside Westminster Abbey – 8,000 as opposed to 20 million - and otherwise heard on radio where it could not of course be seen, and read about in press reports, or watched in local cinemas on newsreel film.

Let's not forget that Queen Elizabeth II came along in Britain's 'television decade' (see chapter four) – the 1950s - which is the first time that general election results were televised, the first time that children's television (including Andy Pandy) was broadcast, the first time that news from Europe was televised, and the first time that a television broadcast from the air was successfully undertaken.

It was also the first time that television cameras entered the Houses of Parliament for a TV broadcast of the opening of a rebuilt chamber.

Lime Grove TV Studios was also opened in the 1950s, which really was a very happening decade for British television, ahead of European television and the rest of the world.

Of course we are talking about black and white television – colour did not follow in the UK until the 1960s – but there would have been no colour without all these black and white developments in TV in the 1950s.

Whilst most of this is not generally understood by today's British public, it will presumably interest them for all that, as they try to get the this year's Diamond Jubilee into an historical perspective, and envisage today's 86-year-old Queen as she was once upon a time, in order to better understand her and the history of her reign better, and it will surely interest foreign visitors likewise, coming to the UK for the Diamond Jubilee.

But, as we shall see in the following chapter, Queen Elizabeth II's relationship with television has by no means been trouble free!

Even so, she has never been anti-television like a goodly number of other royals, royalists and government ministers – on the contrary, as we have seen, she was adventurous enough to resist the temptation to be so back in 1953 – in fact she been quite modernist with regard to television, albeit without recognising some of the negative consequences no doubt.

It was suggested in BBC 2's *100 Greatest Britons* in 2002 that Queen Elizabeth II is not up there with the greatest in the opinion of many people, who voted instead for Winston Churchill in 1st place, which was an excellent choice, of course.

But he was then followed by the likes of Princess Diana in 3rd place before Shakespeare in 5th, Queen Elizabeth Ist in 7th before John Lennon in 8th, Nelson in 9th and Oliver Cromwell in10th and so on.

As we can see from this oddly diverse and weirdly contradictory selection for the top ten greatest Britons of all time, these glorified television straw-polls are certainly not very objective and in many respects they are a bit of a joke – meaningless!

With all due respect to the late Princess Diana and John Lennon, there is no way that they are/were chief among the greatest Britons of all time, greater than such truly great people as Shakespeare and Queen Elizabeth Ist in the case of Princess Diana, or greater than Nelson and Oliver Cromwell in the case of John Lennon!

But, whilst these polls tell us next to nothing about greatness, they do tell us about the crazy perceptions of very different members of the public that get reflected on our television screens. They tell us what some viewers mistakenly think that greatness is and how they define it in populist terms – they also tell us about the climate of opinion and how it has changed, not infrequently for the worse.

Nobody voted for the great people who gave them television in the first place, on which to express their meaningless opinions.

As we see, a great invention may or may not lead to a great result!

I am not suggesting that Queen Elizabeth II should or should not have been included in Britain's top ten or twenty greatest people, only that the selection on offer was a confused and meaningless guide to who exactly great people have been in our history.

Whilst there were some great scientists and inventors in the selection, others were absent, and if for populist and trendy reasons rather than reasons of true greatness, some dubious public figures were included, then there was no reason why Queen Elizabeth II could not have been included (except that nobody responded to the BBC to nominate her for running a great monarchy in their opinion).

Elizabeth's husband, the Duke of Edinburgh, is after all the last royal to have gone into battle during World War Two – when he victoriously commanded his own warship – yet Princess Diana and John Lennon were perceived to be greater than the duke. Obviously, none of this adds up or makes any sense.

I suspect that if viewers had been properly asked to define greatness and to give their reasons for rating their choices, a lot of them would have been disqualified.

But these days a lot of people think that greatness is merely being celebrated as *somebody*, rather than actually doing *something* that overcome a great challenge or solves a great problem, and makes a great difference therefore to the lives and welfare of the greatest number of people, or to great culture, and maybe against great and impossible odds. A lot of people want to be great without *doing* anything great, just as their fans rate them as great, without considering what, if at all, great things they have actually done.

There's no shortage of 100 (and more) great Britons, but it is absurd to think that the late Princess Diana and John Lennon are among them.

In the following chapter we shall see how Princess Diana created a 'great' problem for the Queen of England and her son Charles, as in turn they created great problems for themselves and for her.

Chapter Four

A Fictional Versus a Factual Queen

In the previous chapter it is suggested that the thing to remember about the British royal family is that it is a technological family that is hardly likely, therefore, if only for technological reasons, to turn its back on the scientific wonder of television, and its amazing power for good as a communications tool.

This is a socially informative and reforming tool that has not only liberated British society politically and culturally in a goodly number of ways, but also taken British royalty with it, down its renaissance road. This is why Queen Elizabeth II's decision to embrace television at the outset of her reign, is in my view one of the boldest and profoundly most significant and socially reforming, renaissance things that she has ever done, in her 60 years as Queen of England.

Whilst her astonishing first-ever state visit to Eire, was also significant and bold after all the bloodshed, troubles and hostilities there – another impressive breakthrough for her – that was a one-off on the diplomatic and state visits front, the long-term results of which remain to be seen. But her continuing forays into the world of television have given us one breakthrough after another and another, the results of which have been generally in her favour.

Throughout her reign, one has expected her to do all the usual and very predictable, dutiful and hackneyed routine, show-case, diplomatic and charitable/pr things that royalty always does – with all the traditional trimmings, pageantry and rituals - but to welcome investigative television into her life and do her best to meet it half way, is much more to her credit, it seems to me, than almost anything else she has done, given the risks involved to her mystique and her public image.

This has been very adventurous and bold of her and is a great feather in her cap on the occasion of her Diamond Jubilee.

But, having said that, a love-hate relationship has developed from time to time between the royal family and television, including the rest of the media. – inevitably, no doubt.

However, better a love-hate relationship than no relationship at all, which would of course be a cold war.

After all, there are love-hate relationships in virtually all sectors of society, in and between most families and countries, so these relationships are all perfectly natural and normal are they not? All perfectly inevitable.

They have a history all their own and are a consequence of history and, if we are grown up, we all have to make the most of such relationships and do our best to make them work (especially when they are failing!), which the Queen of England has done her best to do with British television.

Love-hate relationships are a family thing – domestically, nationally and internationally – and they have come into play between British royalty and British television.

But this is not to say that some members of royalty are not still reasonably well disposed towards television and the media, because they are.

Of course, some are definitely not, chief among whom are Prince Philip the Duke of Edinburgh, his daughter Princess Anne and her brother Prince Andrew, whose well-reported grumpy utterances in previous years have made it perfectly clear that they generally have no time for the media and regard it, at best, as the worst of all possible necessary and tedious evils, even though they may have occasionally participated in television programmes over the years.

On the other hand, Queen Elizabeth and her son Prince Charles have been reasonably well disposed to and less openly critical of the media, as have the latest young princes, William and Harry (sons of Charles and the late Princess Diana).

So there is an apparent split in the royal family between those who generally despise and detest television and the media, much of the time, and those who do not.

I was presented to Princess Anne on one notable occasion in the recent past – as a member of Convocation at the University of London of which she is the Chancellor, and also as one of a reception party to help show her round some new university premises – when she snorted 'once a journalist, always a journalist,' after she discovered that I was a former journalist in early retirement.

Her attitude was instantly hostile, even before she got a chance to know who I was or what I did or had done.

Famous for telling journalists and press photographers to 'naff off,' as and when the spirit moves her, and for having said that she does not like royal walkabout (with their common/personal touch) Princess Anne does not mince her words.

But when - much to the horror of others in her university reception party - I unhesitatingly replied, 'yes, once a journalist always a journalist must be a bit like being a princess,' she looked as though she had certainly expected me to hold my tongue and to defer to her.

She instantly glared daggers at me for a brief while - with one of those 'off with his head' facial expressions - but then she suddenly giggled and moved on without further comment, leaving those professors and others who had looked horrified by my reply, to take a big sigh of relief!

I mention this because I think that it gives us a fleeting but revealing insight into her character, personality and attitude – nothing more than a brief insight, but a useful one for all that, for those who have to deal with her, or otherwise assess her, especially if they happen to be despised journalists.

Princess Anne never went to university with her two A-levels, but she likes being Chancellor of the University of London, and she presumably liked being BBC television's *Sports Woman and Sports Personality of the Year* in 1971, for her sporting achievements as a competitive horsewoman, otherwise she would not have turned out to accept her award at the annual televised ceremony.

She also appeared on the long-running television quiz programme *A Question of Sport* as a panellist, where she did a sit-about rather than a despised walkabout.

In 1976 she became the first member of British royalty to compete in the Olympic Games in Montreal in Canada where she succeeded in falling off her horse and getting concussed. But she is a good sport and a good horsewoman, with gold and silver medals from the 2005 European Eventing Championships when she was only 21 years of age, and she has a similar collection of gold and silver medals from equestrian events in the UK.

A pupil of the Spanish Riding School in Vienna, she is second in line to the throne, after her brother, Prince Charles.

But, clearly, this not infrequently prickly Princess is not, like her father before her, one of the royals best disposed to the media or to its television and other news journalists.

HRH Prince Charles, on the other hand, is in my experience a different kettle of fish entirely.

When I interviewed him for a military history of Britain's Gurkha soldiers that I wrote in 2003, his office told me that he could not be interviewed because he only gives one interview per year and had already given a television interview to David Dimbleby of *Panorama* fame.

But I replied, given that Charles was the figurehead Colonel-in-Chief of Britain's Royal Gurkha Rifles, it seemed to me that he had a duty to these soldiers to be interviewed in a book about them, the first, in fact, to feature ethnic Gurkhas officers, rather than restricting itself to the white officer class, like all previous military history books.

There was also the consideration that – unlike *Panorama* current affairs viewers – virtually all Gurkhas and their ethnic and white officers were staunch royalists *par excellence*!

In the case of *Panorama*, less than half or maybe only one quarter are staunch royalists

When my comments were passed on to Prince Charles, word came back that he would be interviewed by email, faxing his replies to any question that I cared to email him. So I sent him a great many questions and finished up with an entire chapter in my virtual interview with him, which was very well received in ethnic Gurkha and military communities in Britain.

Following this, I received a letter from Prince Harry when he was at Eton College, thanking me for a copy of my book that had been sent to him by my publisher. But when I advised Prince Harry to go into the Gurkhas instead of the Blues & Royals, because the Gurkha food (curry) was so much tastier, he politely declined, but not without thanking me for advising him on the subject of his career!

Given that British royals are not accustomed to taking no for an answer, they can hardly complain if others don't take no for an answer from them, and in my experience, they don't mind a spirited reply to them, which may or may not get one anywhere, but it's worth a try. They are supposed to be in the service of their people, after all.

Whilst, generally speaking, authors have no need to intrude upon the stories, lives and histories they have to tell about other people - by including events and experiences from their own lives in those stories - the exception is, it seems to me, when they have personal experiences and insights of their own to offer that are relevant to the telling of the story and can therefore enrich it. I am attempting to do this in this book, when mentioning my own experiences in passing, as and when appropriate.

Obviously, if an author has some personal experience of the people involved, it should add value.

When Queen Elizabeth II had 8,000 VIP guests inside Westminster Abbey to watch her coronation back in 1953, Buckingham Palace did not have enough royal coachmen to transport them all, so country squires and millionaire businessmen turned out for British royalty and dressed up as coachmen to help out.

They were falling over themselves to join in the fun!

Queen Elizabeth II was, at the outset of her reign, billed as a New Elizabethan who was very much in touch with a new world, not the out of touch old world that had gone before, and she was to be a very different kind of monarch from those that had gone before, a new-look monarch for an increasingly new-look modern world and television age.

This was supposed to be a world in which she would reach out to everyone in her kingdom and beyond her shores, with the aid of television, which she would embrace for the first time at her early 20th century coronation in 1953.

As already noted, she would also invent the first family reality-TV programme and follow with a second later on, the final details of which we shall come to in chapter five.

When Queen Elizabeth decided, back then, that her people were as entitled as the charmed inner circle of 8,000 inside Westminster Abbey, to attend her coronation by osmosis, as it were, on their television screens, she also decided that if her monarchy lost some of its mystique, so be it.

With a visual and social infusion of two different fluids/breeds – the royal and the un-royal, those inside the Abbey and outside it, inside the country and outside it – through the porous partition of the television screen, osmosis was being achieved for royalty and the fans of royalty.

Television would be a first for her family and for Westminster Abbey.

On her watch, hers would be a futuristic monarchy with far less mystique than before, which is what it has become today in the 21st century, as she celebrates her Diamond Jubilee in 2012.

She alone has permitted and encouraged this.

Of course, a lot of water has gone under the bridge since she came to her throne and she first let the television cameras into her life and all the other the lives of different members of the British royal family.

Hers was a bold decision back in 1953 – when she could just as easily have listened to her establishment advisers and kept the television cameras out (for a while at least) - and on her head be it that British royalty has lost most of it mystique today, just as her advisors warned her that it would.

But given that royal mystique was already becoming increasingly obsolete, she could see what others who were bending her ear could not see - that it would be better for royals to join the television club instead of trying to ignore it.

No doubt she could see it all coming, worts and all, but had the good sense to move with the times in order to swim with the tide and survive thereby (mixing her metaphors in the process!), and to see if she could contain television in some way.

Perhaps she thought that she could control television and dictate her own terms, which we now know that she could not. No doubt she regrets some if not much of the lost mystique, as her family's dirty linen is repeatedly aired in public in ways that she did not envisage.

Perhaps she hoped to be able to control the big-beast television more than she and Buckingham Palace have been able to do on several notable occasions when the intrusive television cameras have exposed members of her family and called British monarchy to task.

This happened not least at the death and funeral of Princess Diana in 1977 when Queen Elizabeth and her family ran for cover to Scotland.

But they could find no hiding place up in Scotland away from the television cameras that were demanding to know daily why Elizabeth was not showing more concern for the death of her grand daughter, who had recently divorced her son and heir apparent, Prince Charles.

But for all this, no doubt, back in 1953, Queen Elizabeth understood (or had a vague idea) that, like it or not, British monarchy had a better chance of surviving with the roller coaster of television than without it.

It is impossible, today, to imagine a royal family that never or hardly ever appears on television yet still keeps the support and keen interest of its people. Not just its own people, but millions and billions of people of the far-flung world, in several parts of which the Queen of England reigns supreme, as the best-known person in the world.

She is better known and probably has a greater following than the Pope in Rome, all of which is largely due to television and to Queen Elizabeth having welcomed television into her life, with its pesky double-edged sword.

These days, whilst television remains very much largely in favour and on the side of monarchy, this is chiefly on television's own terms, not on the terms of the British monarchy. It is television that calls the shots, not the royal family. On the other hand, television rates monarchy because it is, with common consent, a very classy act with the power to draw millions of viewers.

The love of British television for British royalty in order to attract these viewers and to push up its ratings – like the love of Britain's royalists for British royalty and indeed of royalty for the millions of fans that television can deliver – is a love that is no longer an unconditional one-way love, as it was in the early days of televised royalty in the 1950s when royals called the shots.

Today there is a vicious circle in this *ménage a trios*!

One moment things are gelling, in favour of royalty, other times not, sometimes there is harmony, other times there is disharmony.

But today, television is longer prepared to accept the traditional mystique of yesteryear that existed when Queen Elizabeth II first came to her throne, a once upon a time mystique that most people in Britain today cannot possibly imagine.

With the transparency of television, one simply cannot have televised mystique!

When the full force of intrusive television and the rest of the British media was jointly mobilised against Queen Elizabeth II and her family for their arguably shabby treatment of the late Princess Diana - that appalled the nation - it will have dawned upon Her Majesty big time what she had done by letting television into her life (not that she could have stopped it, not that there was any turning back now).

She will have realised this especially at the Princess's death on August 31st, 1997, and subsequent funeral in September of that year, which is when Buckingham Palace initially declined to respectfully fly its flag at half mast for Dianna, or to give its blessing to a state funeral, or to make a public statement of regret, as the Queen and her family ran off to Scotland with Diana's motherless sons, hopefully beyond the glare of the television cameras (fat chance!) and refusing to return to London.

Princess Diana, divorced from Prince Charles, had earlier run off to Paris with her lover Dodi Fayyad, where she swiftly died in a tragic car crash in an underground tunnel, when she and Dodi were being relentlessly pursued by the paparazzi on motorbikes, and when the French driver of her getaway car was allegedly drunk.

Here was a tragedy of truly Greek proportions.

Previously, Diana had got up royal noses by flouting her differences with her husband Charles and by her apparent indifference to the royal family and to the televised anti-royal consequences of the public scandal.

She had also got up royal noses on account of her affairs with other men, and no doubt for insisting on a massive divorce settlement to the tune of some £19 million. She had brought a lot of scorn and adverse publicity on the British monarchy, making dramatic television that reflected badly on the royals in the minds of many if not most people in Britain and abroad.

Queen Elizabeth will surely have been painfully reminded at this time of how better she and her monarchy would have fared with public opinion in the old secretive days of non-televised royal mystique, when it was anybody's guess what the royal family was up to behind the scenes, and when it did not need too much public approval to carry on as before, without learning the error of its ways, or changing its ways.

In those distant times, most things royal happened behind locked doors and were absolutely hushed up when things went wrong, or were not very flattering or complimentary to royalty, and these matters seldom got into the media, which is why the British public was kept massively and mostly in the dark.

But with the acceleration of a new television age - that came with Britain's New Elizabethan Queen in the 1950s - those days were soon to be long gone, and all British royals would have to answer to public opinion and to television on behalf of the people, if and when royal conduct was questionable, or otherwise not good enough.

At the time of Princess Diana's death, Queen Elizabeth II and her family were eventually forced to fly the flag at half mast for Diana at Buckingham Palace and to return to London from Scotland against their will and make an expression of grief in favour of Diana against their better nature and judgement, all of which they did with the greatest reluctance.

They had absolutely underestimated the huge popularity of Princess Diana and the public's sympathy for her, as well as the power of television to call them to task.

This is all very well documented in and the subject of an academy award winning fictional/factional film in 2006 entitled *The Queen*.

In this film, Helen Mirren plays Queen Elizabeth II brilliantly, just as Alex Jennings plays Prince Charles with great distinction and Michael Sheen plays prime minister Tony Blair no less brilliantly, showing how Blair had no choice but to father the nation, as he made excuses for British royalty, whilst they all ran for cover.

Tony Blair was, it seems from this carefully researched film, pro-royal, whilst his wife, Cheri Blair, was anti.

The Queen was written by Peter Morgan – son of a German Jew in London called Morgenthau who had fled from Hitler's Germany during World War Two and married a Catholic Polish woman who had fled from the Soviet Union to London. Peter Morgan, having written the television drama *Frost and Nixon*, was a good choice to write *The Queen*, and Martin Sheen who had played David Frost in *Frost and Nixon*, was a very good choice to play Tony Blair.

In *The Queen*, the Queen Mother – the late Elizabeth II's mother – was played by the once upon a time slim and shapely young blonde beauty, Sylvia Syms, of *Ice Cold in Alex* fame back in 1958, in which she co-starred with John Mills, just five years after the young Elizabeth II's coronation (Sylvia had also starred in *No Trees in the Street* in 1959 and *The Tamarind Seed* in 1974).

Like Queen Elizabeth II in the 1950s, Sylvia Syms had been a stunning and refined beauty – a typical blonde English rose in Sylvia's case – as opposed to the overweight old lady that she played in the *Queen* film, as an ancient Queen Mother, and she, too, played her part with distinction.

I well remember both Sylvia Syms and Queen Elizabeth II from the 1950s for two very different reasons.

Firstly, Sylvia Syms helped me launch a teenage publication in Reading, my aforementioned home town in the Southeast of England, entitled *Voice of Youth*.

This was when I was just 16 years of age in 1955, and Sylvia helped to launch my publication by writing a letter of goodwill and also autographing one of her pin-up photographs, both of which appeared on the front cover of the launch edition. This was a publication for 6th form college and university students in the town, young nurses in the local nurses home, and any members of the public that were interested to buy a copy for 4 pence, especially football supporters entering Reading Football Club on a Saturday afternoon where it was on offer to them

I appeared on a television youth programme called *Focus on Youth* at that time to talk about my publication in interview with the late Robert Robinson and the London-based Russian editor of the communist *Pravda* newspaper who said that such a publication would not be allowed in the Soviet Union where they did not believe in the cult of youth that was being promoted in Britain and the West.

This was two years after the coronation of Queen Elizabeth II, an event that I had watched previously as a 14-year-old schoolboy on my parents' television set, together with relatives without television sets of their own, who crowded into our house for the occasion.

The year following the coronation, I won a *Queen Elizabeth II Coronation Prize* for outstanding school children in 1954, which is the second reason I have for remembering and personally experiencing these events.

Again, we see what was going on in the country at the grass roots at the outset of Queen Elizabeth's reign.

Her prize to schoolchildren was a book token that I took to WH Smith in Broad Street, Reading, to purchase *100 Great Lives* by Odham's Press, and an Oxford University Press *Road Atlas of Britain*, on both of the covers of which the head and shoulders of Queen Elizabeth II was embossed in bright gold.

As a young schoolboy I was interested to read about the great men and women of history and how they had made something of themselves by doing great things (as I intended to do!) and also to read road maps for my cycling journeys and holidays. Most children could not afford holidays other than cycling holidays, staying in youth hostels, in those days, unless they went to stay in caravans with their parents. This is how things were in Queen Elizabeth II's Britain in those early days.

A book token from the monarch may not sound much of a prize today, but it meant something back then.

Interestingly, Prince Philip, as an officer cadet, had also won a book token at Dartmouth College in 1939 – as it happens, the year of my birth on 11.9.39 at the beginning of World War Two - for being the best all-round cadet of his intake. And this is interesting for the 'all-round' emphasis that was generally an essential requirement for both these prizes, his during the year of my birth, and mine 15 years later in 1954 during the year that followed his wife's coronation.

The traditional emphasis in those distant times was for young people to be all-rounders, rather than specialists, in their academic and other abilities, as well as in their character development.

Yes they were required to be good academically, but they also had to be good at sport and to be public spirited in one way or another, rendering some kind of service to the community.

My prize that was given to mark the occasion of the coronation, was given for the best all-rounders who distinguished themselves on the sports field and in the community, in addition to doing well in the classroom.

In my case I was a house captain, with my house colours in all the sports - in some of which I had represented my school at the county and national level - whilst also writing a couple of school plays for the local community, as well as coming top of the form in several subjects.

Another young school child at that time, in Liverpool, had won a *Coronation Prize* for writing the best essay on the subject of Queen Elizabeth II.

His name was Paul McCartney of future Beatles' fame!

So, when *The Queen* film arrived half a century later, there were two very different memories for me here, in response to this film, memories that provide us with a picture of what was going on in the immediate aftermath to Queen Elizabeth's coronation.

Michael Sheen was a natural to play Prime Minister Tony Blair in *The Queen* because he had previously played Blair in *The Deal* on Channel Four television and in *The Special Relationship* (between Blair and Bush and Britain and the United States). *The Deal* was a television drama about the deal that Tony Blair and his successor, prime minister Gordon Brown, had struck in the Granita restaurant in Islington in North London, which, as it happens, was owned by a neighbour of mine at the time (the restaurant is no more). The Queen of England was born in 1926 in a posh part of London's Mayfair in a town house that is a very fashionable and expensive Chinese restaurant these days!

In *The Queen*, as in real life, Queen Elizabeth and her family ran for cover in order to flee from the ugly reality of Princess Diana's death and the allegedly unkind and arguably callous way in which they had treated Diana, all of which was being reflected on television news daily. The Queen, her husband Prince Philip and the Queen Mother took Diana's two sons – the princes William and Harry – with them to Balmoral.

But British royalty was seriously humiliated and taught a painful and chastening lesson by television on this occasion – and later on by this *Queen* film, almost a decade later - as the shocking Diana news in 1997 was televised to millions, with the opinion polls suggesting that 70% of the British people had turned against the Queen and her monarchy over its unacceptable (to the nation) treatment of Princess Diana, and its apparent indifference to her death and funeral arrangements, and that 1 in 4 wanted the monarchy abolished.

But it transpired that they only wanted it abolished for an hour or two!

They only wanted Queen Elizabeth to turn out and do the decent thing.

Because the 70% that had turned against her back then are back to 80% in her favour now - whilst more than 50% do not want the monarchy abolished - it seems that not too much harm was done to the monarchy over the Princess Diana fracas, that the damage was short lived.

The powder keg was, it seems, damp.

As we see – and as politicians and no doubt the royal image makers know – the public is forever fickle.

But suddenly it had looked as thought television might be a nail in the Queen Elizabeth's coffin, she who had previously invented televised royalty at the time of her coronation, when she could easily have said no to letting the cameras into her life, and kept them away from royalty for at least another five or possibly ten or more years.

How ironic was that?

For sure, television had become a thorn in the Queen's flesh when a defiant Princess Diana appeared on the scene in the 1970s, and then when the princess died, never before had such a damning condemnation of British royalty been presented on the nation's television screens, day after day, until a dithering Queen and royal family backed down and did as they were told by the nation, represented chiefly and almost entirely by television.

At her 1953 coronation Queen Elizabeth II could have had no idea that this was what was meant by the end of her royal mystique, if she let those pesky television cameras into her life.

She could not have had the remotest idea of the consequences of her decision to let the cameras in and to play along with them, or of the consequences of the television age in which she would be embroiled.

The highly publicised and royally unpleasant events immediately following Princess Diana's death, really are well documented in *The Queen* film, which reveals the behind the scenes arguments and strong differences of opinion between the Queen and her son Prince Charles about whether or not Princess Diana's death should be a private or public affair and treated as a royal death or not.

In this remarkably accurate film Queen Elizabeth and her husband Prince Philip wanted a funeral for Diana that was private affair that was quite definitely not to be treated as a royal death with a state funeral and with no public expression of grief from them therefore.

But Prince Charles did not agree, nor did Prime Minister Tony Blair and his government, nor did 70% of the British people.

To have all this aired on television and then subsequently turned into a film was a devastating blow to British royalty.

With the success of this 2006 *Queen* film, the fictional Queen, Helen Mirren, was offered an invitation to dinner at Buckingham Palace in 2007 that she rejected.

This was when the British public was treated to the spectacle of a fictional Queen Elizabeth II, declining to meet and dine with a factual Queen Elizabeth II and her family!

The beautiful and graceful Helen Mirren was a perfect choice to play Queen Elizabeth II, having played two queens in films before – Elizabeth Ist in a film of that title and Queen Charlotte in *The Madness of King George* – and having to her credit 1 Academy Award for Best Actress, 4 Baftas, 3 Golden Globs, 4 Emmys and 2 Cannes Film Festival Best Actress awards. If she is not Britain's very best and most talented actress it is hard to know who is, the Queen of British theatre no less.

As a former Shakespearean actress who has played Lady Macbeth and many other Shakespearean roles besides, she has learnt her craft the hard way and really knows how to act intelligently and well, and she has also played so many roles from the very best drama of classical English and Russian/European literature, including Racine's *Phaedra* at the National Theatre, in addition to all her popular stuff for British television, most notably the female detective in chief of the award-winning series *Prime Suspect*.

She has an intelligently beautiful face – not the usual conventional good looks – that is full of character and she has a subtle charm and grace all her own.

As it happens, she comes from quite a royalist background on her father's White Russian side of her family, because her grandfather was a Tsarist Colonel called Miranoff who finished up as a London cabbie after fleeing from the Russian Revolution and falling on hard times, with a family to support.

He had previously been a diplomat in charge of arms deals in Britain before the revolution came along and he married an East End girl from West Ham who was one of 14 children and whose grandfather had been a butcher to Queen Victoria once upon a time.

The family name Miranoff was changed to Mirren and the Tsarist Colonel's son, Helen's father, played viola in the London Philharmonic Orchestra before World War Two.

Helen was born in Chiswick in West London, but brought up by her parents in Essex in Leigh-on-Sea and also Westcliffe-on-Sea (where, as it also happens, I learnt to swim during a school holiday), and she went to high school in Southend-on-Sea before joining the National Youth Theatre in London and playing Cleopatra at the Young Vic before she was only 20 years of age.

There is a wax-works model of Helen Mirren in London's Madam Tussauds – reportedly at a cost of £150,000 – and like British royals, Helen has all the appearances of being a very forthright and dignified person who, with common consent, has played Queen Elizabeth II accurately and superbly, capturing her mannerisms and facial expressions brilliantly.

But unlike British royals, Helen is a self-proclaimed atheist, so in real life, it seems unlikely that these two Queens would be to each other's taste.

'Queen' Helen told *Esquire Magazine* (August 2011) 'I don't believe in God' but 'I am quite spiritual,' and she doesn't believe in royal honours either, which is why she turned down an OBE, before being persuades by her colleagues to accept it later on in 2003 when she commented that Prince Charles was 'very graceful' but that he forgot to give her half her award – the star – until somebody reminded him!

Unlike the Queen of England, Helen is a liberated feminist – who reportedly confesses to having been date-raped as a student and to having taken cocaine in the 1980s – and it would hardly be surprising, in view of her feminist views, if she had been in absolutely sympathy with and on the side of the self-liberated late Princess Diana, rather than the factual Queen Elizabeth II and British monarchy, with whom it is perhaps likely that she was out of sympathy on this issue (not unlike prime minister Tony Blair's wife, Cherie Blair, in *The Queen* film, played very well indeed by Helen McCory).

It would also hardly be surprising if this is why this fictional queen of stage and film rejected overtures from monarchy's factual Queen to dine at the palace, not that these were the reasons that the fictional queen gave.

She declined dinner at Buckingham Palace on the grounds that she had other filmic commitments in the United States, where, when she had been presented with her best actress Oscar for playing the Queen of England, she praised her (if only for pr purposes in a country and an American profession that is generally pro British royalty!).

But it really would not be surprising if Helen Mirren had been among the 70% or 1 in 4 who were not best pleased with the Queen of England over the treatment of Princess Diana both before and after her death.

Of course one can only surmise and logically deduce these things, but there is always a place in history for reasoned logical deduction.

Even is Princess Dianna had borderline personality-disorder issues – as alleged – the way in which she had been treated by Prince Charles and his mother and father (who allegedly forced this incompatible and loveless marriage upon their son), left very much to be desired and the British public was not impressed!

But this year – during the Queen's Diamond Jubilee celebrations – more than 50% of her people are now in her favour again and the 1 in 4 who wanted her out when Princess Diana died are no longer a problem because the other 3 in 4 are turning out to flag-wave and celebrate the Queen's Diamond Jubilee and cheer her on. And most of the people who wanted her out for an hour or two (70%) are suitably silent.

All Queen Elizabeth had to do, to calm things down over the death of Princess Dianna, was to about-turn, do the decent thing by Diana, and dutifully turn out for the television cameras and meet the public's demands.

For them to forgive her and want her and her monarchy to remain in tact at the top of the tribal totem poll, this is what she did, in order to make everybody happy again.

Unlike her daughter Princess Anne, she did not tell her critics or British television to 'naff' off.

Because, when she first came to her throne, most of her working-class subjects could not afford television sets, as they can of course today, an estimated 3 million people – approximately half the population of London in those days! - lined the streets of the capital city in 1953 to glimpse her golden carriage as it passed by en-route to Westminster Abbey.

She later appeared on the now-familiar and regularly televised Buckingham Palace balcony to be seen in close-up there by an estimated 20 million viewers in Britain and abroad (mostly middle and upper class), for the very first time for a British monarch.

She had well and truly arrived in a television age to become a television queen and, as the celebratory fireworks went off, they went off in more ways than one for her and her family, where the long-term consequences of television were concerned.

Doubtless without realising it, she had taken on more television responsibilities that she realised, and also without realising that she had a tight-lipped silent oath to swear to television, additional to the oath that she had sworn to her people.

With the advent of television, the days of take it or leave it royalty and governments were to be long gone. Both would be relentlessly scrutinised, criticised and paraded on television like never before, and the Queen would be cast in lead roles, either as a national treasure, or as a wicked witch on the occasion of Princess Diana's death, or as a reality-TV queen.

This year, the year of her Diamond Jubilee, will be celebrated and applauded like never before, as she is cast as a national treasure once again, a real-life fairy tale Queen once more.

Chapter Five

Britain's Television Decade

In previous pages reference has been made to Queen Elizabeth coming to her throne during a famous television decade in Britain.

But what decade was that (I hear you ask)?

The 1950s was the decade of television milestones and not least in Britain where television was invented marginally ahead of the rest of the world and where public television was rapidly and substantially developed ahead of it also.

British television became the model for European and World television, especially in its news coverage, the arts, culture and entertainments, and it all began in the early 1950s, which is when Queen Elizabeth II's reign began. She grew in experience and stature in amongst so many new and exciting TV things happening under her nose that she could not fail to be influenced by them. They were all television firsts in the UK and they all came about in the 1950s, as did she, Britain's new television queen in 1953.

There was, in the fifties decade, the *What's My Line* quiz programme in 1951, the British government's first televised budget broadcast in 1953, along with the televising of Elizabeth's coronation in 1953 and the first current affairs news programme *Panorama* in 1953 still going to this day. There were also the first rugby, football and cricket TV broadcasts that year, not to mention the scary *Quatermass Experiment* with its science fiction invasion of earth by aliens from out of space.

In the following year, the first weather forecast came in 1954, as did Richard Attenborough's first animal programme – *Zoo Quest* - and George Orwell's novel, *1984*, prophesying the politically correct manipulation and ultimate state control of all thought and speech and publishing and television.

Clearly, Queen Elizabeth's kingdom and its subjects were being radically changed and much better informed and forewarned by television, for the first time in history.

In 1955, came that loveable and gentlemanly copper in *Dixon of Dock Green*, as did the first *Brains Trust*, *This is Your Life* and *Life with the Lyons*.

By 1956, there was the first ministerial TV broadcast by a government ministers (Anthony Eden), the very funny *Hancock's Half Hour*, the *Billy Cotton Band Show* and the first *Eurovision Song Contest*.

Britain and its people and its monarch would never be the same again.

Thanks to television, everybody was learning a lot more about everybody else, instead of being left in the dark as previously – about royals, government ministers, celebrities, entertainers, clever and brainy people, and then there was pop music in 1957 and 1959 with *Six Five Special* and *Duke Box Jury* respectively.

It was in 1957 that the nation received the first televised *Queen's TV Broadcast* and the her first *Christmas Speech* – two more firsts for Queen Elizabeth II, in addition to her coronation – with the first *Pinky & Perky* children's programme the same year, followed in 1958 by *Blue Peter* and the first *Grandstand* for horse racing enthusiasts, including the Queen of England with her racing horses, of course. *The Sky At Night* and the hilarious *Benny Hill Show* also came in 1957, as did the first Scottish TV Service.

As we see, the 1950s really was the decade of television, in which so many of the first great programmes were born, as television spread like wildfire.

Her father, George VI, had reigned for only 16 years when he died in his sleep in February 1952, which is when she succeeded him, with her coronation that followed in 1953.

At her coronation, the four symbols of her authority – the orb, the sceptre, the rod of mercy and the ring of sapphires and rubies – were all presented to her, with the crown placed upon her head, as their televised images were flashed across the country and around the world.

There had been nothing before like it, either in embryonic television history, or indeed in royal constitutional history.

Britain's first television queen had arrived.

Chapter Six

Inventing The First Family Reality-TV Show

As we have seen thus far in this book, Queen Elizabeth II's is the story of a queen who was light years ahead of her government and other royals where television was concerned at the outset of her reign 60 years ago.

The reasons why few people today realise the television background to Queen Elizabeth II, is either because they are not old enough to remember, or because they have not read about it, or if they are old enough to remember, then it is because most of them have forgotten it in the passage of time – 59/60 years - between 1952/3 and 2012.

I remember it vividly and am doing my best to tell it vividly.

This book not only tells readers about the fascinating history of television, but also about the equally fascinating and lesser-known involvement of Queen Elizabeth II in the promotion of television by royal association throughout her reign.

One of the least recognised/most easily overlooked things about Queen Elizabeth's television history is that she invented the first family reality-TV show in Britain and the United States where there were no such shows previously.

She did this in a 1969 controversial BBC television film entitled *Royal Family* that was hailed as a sensation, because it was the first time that Buckingham Palace had opened its doors to the televisions cameras, allowing them to televise the Elizabeth and her husband Prince Philip at home with their children, Prince Charles and Princess Anne.

Had she not opened the palace doors allowed the cameras to film her and her family at home, the world's first family reality-TV show would not have been invented with the words that she and her family spoke and the domestic actions that they took.

Because this was a posh reality-TV show, with brass knobs on – and most people today think of reality-TV as being anything but posh and quite of often vulgar - most people have not cottoned on to the fact that it was a reality-TV show for all that.

It was intended as the prosaic reality of royals (if such a prosaic thing could possibly exist, as millions of TV viewers were dying to find out!).

Following the broadcast of *Royal Family* by the BBC, it appeared a week later on ITV, providing the British public with an unprecedented through the key-hole glimpse – a fly on the wall glimpse - into the private domestic world of the royals.

This was a ground-breaking TV film in the days before family reality-TV, which did not begin in Britain or the United until the 1970s.

Having sanctioned the televising of her coronation in 1953, Queen Elizabeth II had moved on to invent the first reality-TV programme in Britain and the US on the subject of a family at home in their natural habitat and a royal family at that.

This was five years ahead of the first reality-TV show of an ordinary working-class British family in Reading, some 40 miles to the west of London, called *The Family*, also by the BBC.

Again we see how Queen Elizabeth II was ahead of the game in these television developments.

It was also a couple of years ahead of the first US reality-TV show, called *An American Family*, in 1971. This show chronicled the breakup of the Loud family and the divorce of Bill and Pat Loud, introducing viewers to their gay son.

Whilst the Buckingham Palace show was reality-TV with brass knobs on, the working-class family show that followed it in the UK was as anything but!

It was based on a loud-mouthed and very common, rough and ready family called the Wilkins, who swore and cursed and had their trivial family rows televised from inside their cramped and insalubrious flat over a greengrocer's shop in a grotty part of town.

Mr Terry Wilkins was a Reading bus driver and his wife Margaret was a real finger-wagging and quarrelsome battle-axe who repeatedly told her husband and four children 'do it my way or you'll be sorry' (no doubt Queen

Elizabeth takes a similar view, albeit not expressed so aggressively or uncouthly!).

For six months the TV cameras were in the Wilkins' flat recording virtually everything, and after the series, Mr and Mrs Wilkins' marriage broke up and a remarried. Mrs Wilkins is now dead, having died of a heart-attack in the 1980s.

The Wilkins family was billed as 'the kind of people who never get on television' (and a lot of people said thank goodness for that, get them off now!).

By contrast the British royal family were the kind of people who got on television all the time and couldn't get enough of it as they welcomed the cameras into their living quarters. They were important people, the Wilkins of Reading were not, but suddenly they were important on television for a while, and for all the wrong reasons.

But in one sense, the royal family had one thing in common with the Wilkins because, they too, the kind of people who never got on reality-TV – not on television but on reality-TV.

Like the Queen of England, Margaret Wilkins of Reading was short and stocky, but very roughly and loudly spoken and very poor, which was of course quite unlike Queen Elizabeth.

This is how ground-breaking family reality-TV shows were born in Britain and the United States and it was the

British royal family that gave birth to it in Buckingham Palace.

There had been just one reality-TV show about school children growing up in Britain previously, not chronicling the daily domestic affairs of a family, like the Louds, the Wilkins and the British royal family - but about some schoolchildren growing up and what they had achieved when they became adults years later – but this was not a reality-TV study of a family in its own home.

So this did not quite count as the first reality-TV show about a single adult family and its children.

Most television viewers today are familiar with realtiy-TV of all sorts, involving ordinary and anonymous people, celebrities and well-known people, and some lap it up with great enthusiasm, whilst others deplore it, regarding it as deadly dull and boring dumbing down of the worst possible kind.

But few, if any, realise that this dumbing down was invented by the Queen of England with Britain's first realtiy-TV family show that was filmed inside Buckingham Palace.

Even many of those who make it their business to know about television programmes, do not realise that it was the Queen of England who gave us the first reality-TV family show, not Queen Elizabeth's television counterpart-successor, the late Mrs Margaret Wilkins of Reading.

My late parents were alive and well in Reading in those days and thought the Wilkins an appallingly vulgar family that should never have been put on screen. My parents and a great many others like them could not see that there was anything entertaining or otherwise useful or informative about the show.

The usefulness of reality-TV at Buckingham Palace, by contrast, they could just about understand – given that this was Britain's royal family and millions or ordinary people needed to become familiar with them in order to rally to the royal cause. On the other hand, my parents were apprehensive, because they could not see what was ordinary or ever could or should be ordinary about royalty (which is what the show aimed to demonstrate to whatever extent that was remotely possible!).

Funnily enough, after the show, word got round that Queen Elizabeth II was disappointed with the outcome because it made the royal family look too ordinary!

But the sleazy reality of the Wilkins family went right over their heads. So what if they were ignorant and uneducated quarrelsome people who regularly argued about nothing and verbally abused each other with foul language? What was the point of that? So these people never got on television otherwise, well three cheers for that! What was the point of putting them on television?

The point was supposed to be to remind viewers what they already know, that such ignorant people exist and have a right therefore to do their worst on television. But - how stupid was that? - my parents wanted to know

Because the Wilkins family had no mystique to lose by such a programme, my parents and many others had no interest in them, given that they were only too familiar with people like them, who never got on tele. But, with royal mystique to lose, my parents and others were very interested to penetrate that mystique and find out more about the royals and what they were like behind the scenes.

Three-quarters of the British population reportedly watched *Royal Family* by Richard Cawston, and the programme was replayed time and again on screen during its first year. It was a tremendous success.

But some critics argued that Richard Cawston's film destroyed the mystique of the royals by showing them to be ordinary people, including scenes of the Duke of Edinburgh frying sausages at a Balmoral barbeque!

Given that the royals were anything but ordinary people – mein got! – one could also argue that the *Royal Family* was an insult to viewers' intelligence (not that all or even many television viewers necessarily could care less about having their intelligence insulted).

Just as the critics back in 1953 had been opposed to televising Queen Elizabeth's coronation on the grounds that it would be curtains for traditional royal mystique, 16 years later the critics remained, complaining that television was finally finishing off the mystique of the British monarchy good and proper, and with the consent of Queen Elizabeth.

Royals should not stoop so low in their opinion.

And just as Queen Elizabeth II had not listened back in 1953 about not televising her coronation, again she did not listen in 1969 about not getting into reality-TV, as she opened the gates and the doors at Buckingham Palace to the television cameras, just as she had opened the doors in Westminster Abbey, 16 years previously.

Clearly, Britain's television queen was still in love with television.

Her reality-TV programme showed her making small talk with guests and suggesting to US President Richard Nixon that 'world problems are so complex, aren't they now?

It is said that even Sir David Attenborough, a BBC controller in 1969, allegedly told Cawston that his film was 'killing the monarchy,' not that the Queen seemed to agree with this, or to care very much, except to say that, by the end of 1969, the film was suddenly withdrawn from public view without explanation and it has not been seen again in public since that time – 43 long years ago!

So maybe Queen Elizabeth was finally getting the message about the damage that television could do to her image and her monarchy's previously spell-binding mystique?

Maybe, when she saw the result of the *Royal Family*, she was disappointed?

Perhaps she came to understand her critics who have claimed that this kind of television dumbs royalty down, just as it dumbs televsion down, just as it demeans royalty?

Who knows?

Royal correspondents in the media never ask such delicate questions when interviewing royals. Probably they think they would not get any straight answers if they did.

They ask Prime Ministers – Tony Blair, Gordon Brown, David Cameron – about why they allowed the television cameras into their homes, but not monarchs.

By letting the cameras into her home at Buckingham Palace, Queen Elizabeth had dared to give television the benefit of the doubt once more, as she had done previously at the outset of her reign, which is why she had become Britain's television queen.

But if she was beginning to learn, 16 years later, that she had been wrong, that she ought to have kept the cameras out, as she might have done, then she was beginning to learn the hard way, locking the stable door after the horse had bolted.

The satirical publication, *Private Eye*, has poked fun at British royals, giving them working-class names, presumably to make sport of them for trying to pretend that they are ordinary when they manifestly are not and never can be.

The Queen of England is referred to as Brenda, the Duke of Edinburgh as Keith, the late Princess Margaret as Yvonne, and the late Princess Diana as Cheryl!

But the problem for *Private Eye* is that its editor, Ian Hislop, has also become a media bunny, same as everybody else, and frequently tries to pretend that he is ordinary, rather than privileged, and not quaffing champagne all the time, when he gets into political argument on *Have I Got News for You.*

Having written for and lunched with *Private Eye*, I know that Hislop has his critics who have been less than impressed over the years with his publicity-seeking and self-promotion on television, not to mention his politically slanted satire, very pointedly against some things – such as the left wing, New Labour and the unions – but not against others (such as the right-wing and his dearly beloved Christian religion, a passion for which is one thing that he shares with Brenda).

This year, during Queen Elizabeth's 2012 Diamond Jubilee celebrations, London's National Portrait Gallery has reportedly been given royal permission to show a tiny bit of Elizabeth's once upon a time controversial reality-TV film in a gallery exhibition celebrating the queen's Jubilee.

We are told that the film clip shows the Queen sitting down to breakfast at Buckingham Palace with the Duke of Edinburgh, Prince Charles and Princess Anne, telling them some anecdotal story about a dignitary falling over in front of Queen Victoria.

Because Buckingham Palace has restricted this years' exhibition film-clip from the *Royal Family* to just 90 seconds, the remainder of the documentary remains off-limits to the public, so the public today are none the wiser about what this royal reality-TV show was all about, and why it has been quietly discontinued (but they can guess!) If the full film could be shown again at the National Gallery it would be much more instructive.

Paul Moorhouse, exhibition curator at the National Portrait Gallery, has told the *Daily Telegraph* (January 13th, 2011): "Legend has it that the Queen doesn't want parts of it to be shown. Regrettably, the film hasn't been seen for a long time. It just disappeared. There is a reluctance for this to be revisited. I wish we could show it in its entirety. It tells you a lot about family life. And it redefined the nation's view of the Queen - the audience were amazed to be able to hear the Queen speaking spontaneously, and to see her in a domestic setting.'

And this is the point – television has *redefined* Queen Elizabeth II and her family. By letting the cameras into their lives and becoming TV celebrities, British royals *aint wot they used to be*! They have been changed by television and the queen has been turned into a television queen.

This year's Portrait Gallery exhibition is entitled *The Queen: Art and Image* and it features a variety of very different portraits, photographs and contemporary art works, including Queen images by Cecil Beaton, Pietro Annigoni and Andy Warhol.

According to Paul Moorhouse, the Queen is 'probably the most visually represented person ever to have lived, and yet what do we actually know about her?'

Well, he can say that again, because we really do not know very much, given that the she, like other royals, is not allowed to say very much of consequence, or to tell us her thoughts, so what she is like – for real – has become a national guessing game.

When we say that the queen is the most visually represented person - about whom, arguably, her images tell us next to nothing – what does that tell us?

That she sometimes looks like this or that or something else?

That artists and photographers are falling over themselves to ret-interpret and recreate her image?

That art and image are one thing, whilst substance and the inner person are something else?

That art and image can only provoke thought, but can never properly explain the thought to which it gives rise? That words and books are better than images for interpreting the thought processes of royals and getting into their heads maybe?

For me – and I shall certainly be attending the Portrait Gallery exhibition – painterly and photographic images are very interesting for what they tell us about the magical skills, talents, interpretations and genius of the artists, rather than the subjects in question. It is the artists and their reality and frame of mind that are the key to all this.

We are told that the National's exhibition of the queen's visual images, chronicles the way in which the monarchy has been 'downsized and de-imperialised over the past 60 years,' and this must surely be the case, in view of the tremendous changes in history throughout Queen Elizabeth II's reign in which she, more than any monarch previously, has changed with the changing times.

The exhibition begins, evidently, with her first appearance as Queen of England in February 1952 with her arrival in Britain from Kenya after learning that her father, King George VI, had died.

Pictures from the early years of her reign are said to be those of pomp and ceremony, including Beaton's coronation image from 1953 and Pietro Annigoni's 1955 portrait.

But the organisers tell us that she is also remembered in this exhibition as a beauty in a photograph by Dorothy Wilding, taken in 1952, and used thereafter on stamps, coins and cards (talking of stamps, see the following chapter).

'From this distance,' Paul Moorhouse has told the *Telegraph*, we forget that the Queen entranced the nation with her youth, freshness and glamour.'

We are reminded that because, in the 1960s, there was a general sea-change in the way in which the Queen was portrayed – along with virtually everybody else of note – royal images of her became quite different from before, not that this tells us much about her, but more about a changed public interest in visualising her and also the continuing demand for her in any shape or form.

Her images may have become quite different, but, at heart, has she become different, or is she acting? What has become different is that she is consenting to these different images, but has this basically changed who she is and is she enjoying becoming a changed person? For sure, this is a learning process of her. But does she any longer know who she is in relation to all these different images that she is giving out? Does she care? Do we care and, if so, why? Unless and until she speaks for herself, we shall never know (enter the aforementioned John Humphrys who wants to be the first interview her!)

It seems that, in this exhibition, Buckingham Palace has been keen to emphasise that the queen is a wife and a mother in touch with the real and ordinary lives of her subjects, and to this end the exhibition has a photograph of the Queen cradling the infant Prince Andrew, taken in 1960, without any of the usual trappings of monarchy.

According to Paul Moorhouse, the 1966 Aberfan disaster in Wales was the 'tipping point for the Queen's image. 'She was criticised because she didn't go to Aberfan immediately and there was a sense that she wasn't sufficiently in touch with her people. Her advisers felt this and knew something had to be done. It led to a new way of portraying the Queen as approachable.'

The Aberfan disaster was when a great mountain of coal in Wales slid down from a mighty height on coal miners' cottages and a school underneath, killing a great many children and adults.

Another image - from 1971 - taken by Patrick Lichfield, reportedly reveals the queen laughing in what is described as an off-duty moment as she watches someone being playfully thrown overboard from the Royal Yacht Britannia.

We are told that a contemporary image by Chris Levine in his 2007 portrait, *Lightness of Being*, gives us a queen with her eyes are closed, and that the Queen reportedly told Levine that she loved his picture.

Sandy Nairne, director of the National Portrait Gallery, points out that the 2012 Diamond Jubilee offers us an opportunity to reflect on 'our history, our country and our times."

Readers interested to do this can attend this exhibition that opens at the National Portrait Gallery in London later this year before going on tour to the following venues:

National Gallery Complex, Edinburgh (June 25 - September 18 2011)

Ulster Museum, Belfast (October 14 2011 - January 15 2012)

National Museum, Cardiff (February 4 - April 29 2012)

National Portrait Gallery, London (May 17 - October 21 2012)

Whatever else may be said of Queen Elizabeth II, nobody can seriously accuse her of not going along with the most of demands of television, photography and film, during her reign. One might almost say that she has bent over backwards to comply with the public interest in her and her family – within reason and with one or two exceptions, notably over the dispute with the late Princess Diana and other scandals regarding her children which she has of course tried to keep off limits – and, as we have seen in this chapter, she has been the first to give family reality-TV to the British public in 1969.

Since then, the floodgates have opened to dreaded reality-TV programmes that have positively swamped viewers on both side of the Atlantic in Britain and the United States, and anyone who doubts this has only to google the subject to see how many dozens and hundreds of utterly appalling reality-TV programmes there have been, but who in their right mind would want to do this other than media studies students and researchers?

Ironically, these largely illiterate programmes have become exercises in latter-day media literacy!

And as we have seen in this book thus far, Britain's television queen is both media literate and computer literate (in her use of emails).

She is also knighting Peter Bazalgette this year, for his services to television – he who pioneered much of reality-TV on British television, a good while after she invented it back in 1969, in addition to pioneering his how-to TV programmes.

It was he who first brought *Big Brother* to the UK from Holland, regarded by many as the worst and most vulgar reality-TV show of all, with all its verbally and racially abusive language, and its sex under the bed covers!

As we see, Queen Elizabeth takes everything in her stride, including the dumbest forms of reality-TV, as and when it is required of her.

Chapter Seven

A Queen that Puts Her Stamp on the World

Prior to television, postage stamps were the chief carriers of Queen Elizabeth II's global image to millions of people in different parts of the world, reaching more 'viewers' more regularly – on a daily basis – than radio was able to reach listeners.

In this chapter we see how she has put her stamp on the world.

These miniscule postage pictures were/are royal logos, the sight of which has very probably had a powerful subliminal effect on people over the years.

A suitably repetitive and influential effect, keeping the monarch's image alive and well all over the world in the consciousness of a goodly number of those to have stuck the stamps on letters, as well as those who have received them, whether at home or abroad.

Most multinational companies would jump at the chance of such an effective logo, travelling daily all over different countries and between countries, in and out of the homes and offices of millions of people.

For a small family business, such as the House of Windsor, this was and remains big corporate promotion, which is why of course the British royal family was and remains a massively wealthy small business (almost certainly the wealthiest small business the world).

As can be seen from stamps during Elizabeth II's reign, it is true to say she (like her predecessors before her) has benefited in this way from a penetrating global image promotion, before television arrived on the scene to accelerate it on from there.

By use of stamps, people in different English-speaking countries, and different Commonwealth countries that spoke English as their second language, were kept constantly aware that Elizabeth was their monarch – the Postage Stamp Queen in the days before she became the Television Queen later on.

In the centre pages in this book, there are examples of different stamps promoting different images in different countries, where the British monarch has been marketed in this way, every day of the week and month of the year, year after year (no doubt the royals and the recipient countries in question would not refer to this as marketing or even image promotion).

Stamps in the history of British royalty have been neat and discreet, constant little but powerful reminders, of the allegiance of people outside and also within the UK to British monarchy, whose mystique has been kept going in this way (Andrew Marr's recent *Diamond Queen* book this year, about Queen Elizabeth II, has a postage stamp on the cover).

Interestingly, one of the early British stamps in Queen Elizabeth's reign, has Winston Churchill in the foreground and Elizabeth's head over his shoulder in the background!

Queen Elizabeth and her husband the Duke of Edinburgh had massive respect for Winston Churchill and they turned out for his state funeral at St Paul's Cathedral, but to have a stamp of him with the Queen of England behind him is something else.

The interesting thing about this Churchill stamp is that, because it was he who advised against televising Elizabeth's 1953 coronation on the grounds that television would strip her of her mystique, he can now be perceived in this context as standing in her way. And we are reminded of this by this stamp, in which she is behind him in this postal image, almost as if she is looking over his shoulder.

So this stamp, with Churchill up front, and Elizabeth behind in the top right-hand corner of what is a dual image, is really interesting for its suggestion or implication (with hindsight) of a new young queen coming out of a shadowy and mystical background to overtake the old world and take matters into her own hands; pushing the old world aside in favour of a bright new world of transparent television exposure in which royal mystique is no longer a possibility.

Not that this stamp (included in the centre pages of this book) could possibly have been designed for this purpose, or with this interpretation and perception in mind, but as it happens, this is how things have turned out, giving this particular stamp a new and latter-day symbolism that was not intended at the time.

This is a symbolism that has been bestowed upon it by fate, if you like, and/or by latter-day history.

Of course, stamps are still an important part of conveying the imagery the monarch today regardless of the presence of television – as are currency notes and coins – but before television, the bigger and virtually only part of Elizabeth's global image projection (along with film newsreels that had less exposure).

It really was vividly colourful and detailed little stamps, like messages in bottles, that were floated off to the outside world to carry the message of British royalty to foreign shores, given that the royals could not be seen on radio broadcasts, and not seen every day or even week on film newsreels from or about Britain.

Without doubt, stamps made a very big different to keeping the royal image and influence alive in such places as Saint Lucia, Bahamas, Rhodesia and Nyasland, Zambia, Cyprus, Malta, Australia, New Zealand, Canada, Singapore, Hong Kong and Ceylon, in addition to the UK, to mention but a few places.

Some of these stamps are glamorous, others exotic, with, for example, Queen Elizabeth looking over the grave and tombstone of Cecil Rhodes in Rhodesia, or over the beautiful harbour of Kyrenia in North Cyprus (which is still beautiful to this day), or looking at elephants in Ceylon (these days there would be television images of such things).

Whilst stamps are only a small, foregoing part of the visual imagery and history of Queen Elizabeth II in relation to television, they are a significant part for all that, and worthy of mention in this chapter therefore.

The power of postage stamps to reach millions of people in the UK and throughout the world is not to be underestimated, and in the dark days before television it never was underestimated, because in the absence of TV, it was postage stamps more than anything else that promoted the global image of British monarchs, including Elizabeth II.

Unfortunately these stamps were too small to be properly appreciated for their design detail and content, but in the centre-pages of this book, justice is done to each stamp by enlarging them.

Chapter Eight

The Queen of England as Television Icon

From everything that has gone previously in these pages, it is obvious that Queen Elizabeth II is Britain's longest-surviving television icon in the 20th and 21st centuries.

More than any other TV-icons to which one can refer, her image has been constantly reflected on our television screens and, as we have already seen on the cover of this book, where there is an imitation 1950s image of her on a television screen – making her annual Queen's Speech on Christmas day – a lot of people still think that Christmas is not Christmas without her.

Let's think about that for a moment. For millions of viewers, Christmas would not be the same without her Christmas Day speeches – how many other wannabe TV-icons have had such a long-running iconic success and annual tribute paid to them, year in and year out?

And how many have had their televised images repeatedly reflected for as long as 60 years in so many television news programmes, virtually everywhere they have gone, in addition to the television programmes about her life and times, in all of which her trusty old image has been constantly reflected ?

Of course, her iconography has been reflected elsewhere in the print media, as well as on stamps and coins, bank notes and all sorts of souvenir relics marking different occasions in her life – drinking mugs and glasses, tableware, plaques and so on – and all with the aim of promoting a venerable and near-sacred image of her by which she can be remembered by her fans.

Michael Jackson, Elvis Presley, eat your hearts out!

Since the invention of icons by the image-makers of the world's ancient religions – *eikon* is the Ancient Greek word for image – in Greece, Syria, Egypt and Rome, it is clear that no other single person on this planet, who is neither a saint nor a God, has had so many representational images made for purposes of veneration and image promotion. Let us not forget that Elizabeth's predecessors, who also had their royal icons, did not have television icons/images flying through the air on their behalf, which is why she is of course a television icon as well as a television queen.

Iconographic art today includes television images, along with all the others that went before.

Scientific history was on Elizabeth's side when television came along to accelerate the action for her, and television in the passage of time has proved that the world's religions do not have the moral or intellectual copyright on iconography anymore, as once they did in ancient and/or recent times.

An icon remains, as it always was, any representational image that you care to mention, especially when symbolising the worshipful reverence and/or infatuation shown to certain people and certain happenings and events – holy people and figures once upon a time, but not of necessity anymore.

So religion lost its intellectual copyright on the ideas that icons are supposed to represent, whilst television gradually took over. These are ideas of certain people being sacred, near-sacred or very special and precious indeed.

Whilst the early icons of the Greek and Russian orthodox churches - and also the Roman churches - were often painted on wood, or otherwise reproduced on mosaics, these days they are reproduced on all sorts of materials, and on television they come literally out of thin air, as they are sent on their travels in images that finish up on television screens (unless and until they get switched off!).

But there are on British television today no holy icons as a permanent fixture and, what we have instead are celebrity icons mostly from the world of sport and entertainment, as well as from royalty, among whom Queen Elizabeth II of *House of Windsor* fame is in pride of place.

She is streets ahead of, for example, David Beckham, the TV-icon footballer of *Beckingham Palace* fame, Sir Alan Sugar of *The Apprentice* fame, and Simon Cowell and Cheryl Cole of *X Factor* fame, or Piers Morgan of celebrity-TV interviewer fame.

Thankfully there are, as yet, no reality-TV programmes about the Beckhams at home, Cheryl Cole and her family at home, Simon Cowell and his mum at home – what a relief, one shudders to think! – as there have been about Queen Elizabeth and her family at home, as all these major TV-icons compete with British royals for television celebrity.

Whilst television has given us a glimpse of prime ministers and their families in their homes and/or Downing Street premises – David Cameron, George Brown and Tony

Blair – they have not had anywhere near as much air-time as Queen Elizabeth and her family have had television air-time.

All things considered, there seems to be no doubt that Queen Elizabeth's iconic status on television is far ahead of others.

But this is a status that she has had to earn (and quite right, too, in view of the fact that she is massively privileged and financially provided for in so many super-rich ways), and she has had to earn it because deference to royalty in the UK is, for the most part, long gone, and not least on television (republicans may accuse television of not being critical enough of royalty, but they cannot reasonably accuse it of too much deference anymore). Elizabeth's iconography does not come from the deference of yesteryear that she could certainly have expected, but by public demand.

These days it is she who defers to public demand where television is concered!

She cannot - like the King of Saudi Arabia, for example - order the television channels to run a royally approved film clip, or a head and shoulders pic' of her daily, or to make a programme of her in this way but not that way, for this purpose but not that purpose. Nor can she order television not to televise her when she does not want to be televised, or not to put her in news reports and news programmes when she does not want to be in the news. She cannot order the televised *Spitting Image* puppets of her and her family not to be televised (all she can do is turn the tele' off, or otherwise join in the fun). If she wants a television presence, she must go along with the requirements of television, either the reality-TV requirements, or other requirements. And even if, truth to tell, she would rather not have a television presence, she is going to get one whether she likes it or not!

But, whilst it is television that has put her on the box to make her popular, nobody has put a gun to the heads of millions of viewers who have tuned in to watch. Had nobody watched, she would have been taken off in double-quick time.

Just as nobody has put a gun to the heads of the worshipful fans of David Beckham, Simon Cowell and the rest, nobody puts a gun to the heads of her fans either – television is for consenting adults of all kinds! – but these TV-icons do not get their fans without competing for them and giving them what they want, pretty much on the terms of their fans. If the fans don't want X Factor-type entertainment, then Simon Cowell is not going to make it as a TV-icon, and the same is true of the Queen of England, she has to give her TV fans what they want, including reality-TV and whatever else, within reason, they require.

So Queen Elizabeth has done well to get so much television exposure (on the whole favourable and positive), as she has made her monarchy fit for television purpose, and moved it with the times.

Not that any of this has been a stroll through the park for her because, she has had to work at it – she has had to work at being Britain's television queen.

Even the *Spitting Image* puppets of her and her family have added to her celebrity, even though they have not been to the taste of all her fans (or to the royal family perhaps). Talking of which, I well remember, in my consultancy days, back in the 1990s, suggesting to the head office of

Barclays Bank in the City of London, that they play an April Fools' trick on the *paparazzi* by hiring puppets of Margaret Thatcher and President Reagan for a photo shoot at the opening of a new international branch of Barclays in the new docklands, in east central London, a branch that was in need of promotion – the trick being that photo editors would be invited on April Fools' Day to come and take pics of prime minister Thatcher and President Reagan attending the opening ceremony of the branch because, among other things, the manager wanted to discuss their overdrafts with them!

Which newspapers wouldn't turn out to take photographs of the branch of a bank, if they knew that they were going to get a highly unusual pic' of messrs Thatcher and Reagan together? A newly opened branch that would otherwise not even get a mention in the press, let alone photographs of its area manager (Ted Robins) in the presence of a British prime minister and an American president?

The *paparazzi* immediately recognised their invitation to the branch opening as an April Fools' Day joke, of course, but when they heard what was going on with the puppets, they loved it, and all the national newspapers turned out to take photographs, including the *Financial Times* that was and is not big on photographs in its pink pages.

But one of the head office managers at Barclays thumped his fist on his desk and loudly declared 'I will not have this bank associated with a television programme that regularly insults the Queen of England.'

And a goodly number of other Barclays personnel agreed with him.

That was the strength and solemnity of feeling for Queen Elizabeth and her family among old-style, belt-and-braces bankers (which is the point of this story), representative of former times when such a publicity stunt would indeed have been regarded as 'insulting' to Queen Elizabeth.

Even though it was only the puppets of politicians – rather than Queen Elizabeth and the Duke of Edinburgh that could just as well have been used for this event – that were proposed, the old-school fans of royalty were having none of it.

But the desk-thumper and his sympathisers were overruled by the bank's public relations supremo – James Poole, formerly of the *Sunday Times* – who declared that they were 'old hat' and that most people in 1990s Britain did not regard the *Spitting Image* puppets as insulting to British royalty.

So the event went ahead and was a great public relations success for the bank and not a single pro-royal newspaper objected to a TV programme that poked fun at the royals and satirised them by using grotesque puppets to this end. They all thought it a hoot, deserving of space in their newspapers, including the *Daily Telegraph* whose City Diary ran a jolly little story on the subject of the behind the scenes dispute about whether or not to identify Barclays with a TV programme that was 'insulting to the Queen of England.'

As we see, times have changed drastically in Britain with regard to what is and is not acceptable publicity about British royalty. There has been a great mood-swing away form deference and these are the new-look times with which Queen Elizabeth has had to move in order to keep the British media 'on message' and to become a television icon.

But in this year's *Daily Mail*'s Top 100 British Celebrities who 'really matter' – by television celebrity-interviewer in Britain and the United States, Piers Morgan – she is written off as 'old hat' (Jan 18th 2012), just as her old-school fans were written off as old hat by James Poole and Barclays.

She doesn't tick all the boxes of Piers Morgan's criteria, with the details of which I will not bore readers, although one of which was that celebrities had to be outside politics, as the Queen of England certainly is.

Given that the *Daily Mail's* readers represent Tory middle-England and are no doubt mostly fans of royalty, many of them probably gritted their teeth when they read that the Queen of England had been written off and did not figure even in the Top 100 (or even ten)!

One does not have to agree or disagree with Pier's Morgan's celebrity selection, because the point about it in this book is that it is television 'celebrity' that the royals are up against and with which they must therefore compete and become celebrities themselves if they want to hold their own with other TV-icons.

This is what they are up against as they attempt to make the British monarchy fit for purpose in the modern world, and to maintain a loyal fan base, chiefly through television because it has millions of viewers in contrast to the dwindling thousands of newspaper readers.

The only royal to make it in the *Mail's* top ten – in an impressive 4th place – is the new-look Prince William who is seen as a trendy young royal for the times in which we live, who matters more than the Queen in terms of celebrity.

He is presumably 'new hat,' as he takes to the stage with his commoner wife, Kate Middleton, and his studied Thames Estuary accent (that he shares with his brother Harry) to disguise the fact that he is a royal toff (my observation, not Piers Morgan's or the *Daily Mail's*).

Even so, I'll throw my hat into the ring for Queen Elizabeth II as the longest-surviving and most successful television icon – i.e. a media sacred image on our television screens that gets much more television coverage than previous royals and all others, purely on account of who she is and what she represents.

She also gets coverage elsewhere in endlessly reproduced paintings and/or prints in the art world (as we can see at this year's Diamond Jubilee exhibition at the National Portrait Gallery in London) and on postage stamps (as we have seen in the previous chapter).

The point at which a televised celebrity is elevated to icon status, is interesting and debatable, and some would argue that the Queen of England is an icon with or without television, though I seriously doubt that she would be such a massive icon as she has become with television.

The footballer, David Beckham, has iconic status with millions of football fans, and not least in Japan where he has reportedly been turned into some kind of god (where, by all accounts, there is some kind of sacred statue of him)!

Sir David Attenborough is another possible icon, as suggested by a recent exhibition of his works at the National Portrait Gallery in 2008, where a special photographic portrait of him was unveiled in conjunction with his *Life in Cold Blood* television series.

Hailed as the 'grandfather' of TV nature programmes since his first programme in 1954 – one year after Queen Elizabeth's televised coronation in 1953 – he was chosen as the 'top living icon in a National Portrait Gallery opinion poll in conjunction with BBC2's *Culture Show* (as we see, the worlds of culture and art, and not just the media, sport, pop music and religion, have their respective interests in promoting the idea of icons). Sir David beat, among others, the long-time pop stars, Sir Paul McCartney and David Bowie, the long-time film star Michael Caine, novelist Alan Bennett, singer Kate Bush, television actor, satirical comedian and presenter, Stephen Fry and also Morrissey.

This was reported in the press and not least in *The Independent* newspaper (March 8th, 2008 edition) in an article entitled 'A Portrait to Mark the Selection of Britain's Greatest Icon.'

It seems that, these days, icons are ten a penny and, you *pays your money and you takes your choice*!

But, on reflection, not just these days, because, when we think about it, it was forever thus, even in ancient times, although they were not ten a penny back then, unless they were religious icons.

An icon of British theatre and film is Helen Mirren who played Queen Elizabeth II in *The Queen* film, and Dame Judi Dench, who played Queen Victoria on the cinema screen.

Whilst icons do not need to have a religious or spiritual significance anymore, they do need to be recognised for their quasi-god-like following. They do need to be venerated for whatever reason and by a great many people, which is where television comes in.

In order to make it as a television celebrity or icon, according to Piers Morgan, one has to compete with the likes of: *X Factor* judge and music mogul, Simon Cowell, who is in first place in the *Mail's* list, 'the most important and influential celebrity in Britain right now is The Boss' and he is also 'mischievous, arrogant, funny, vain, cunning and loyal; David Beckham in second place, he of the aforementioned footballing and also 'Beckingham Palace' fame, who has 'spent the decade,' according to Piers, 'promoting himself in one of the greatest and most ruthlessly selfish ego trips in the history of sport;' the pop singer and former *X Factor* judge, Cheryl Cole, in third place, 'the nation's sweetheart after joining *The X Factor* as a judge;' and the Queen's own grandson, the aforesaid Prince William.

Others in the *Mail's* top-celebrity selection include the former Beatles pop-idol, Sir Paul McCartney and his ex-wife Heather Mills (on whom Paul settled a staggering £24 million divorce settlement 'after four years of married hell'); the footballing hard man, Vinnie Jones; the two stand-up comics and *Britain's Got Talent* presenters, Ant and Dec, 'after Simon Cowell they're the highest-paid stars in British TV history' (reportedly Simon Cowell earns an estimated £54 million per annum before tax; Sir Alan Sugar (of *The Apprentice* fame); super models Kate Moss and Naomi Campbell, the latter black model who is 'an impossible little madam' with 'problems with anger management, drugs and time-keeping,' but 'Britain would be a duller place without her;' comedian Eddie Izzard; film and stage actor Kenneth Branagh; long-running pop singer Rod Steward; television game-show presenter Anne Robinson (one of the very first women 'all over TV now');

female novelist of *Harry Potter* fame, J.K. Rowling; television chef Delia Smith.

Then there is the ubiquitous Sir David Attenborough who, as already noted, is a television celebrity and icon from way back, from the 1950s to the present day.

Whilst I would not touch half of these with a barge pole – and only three or four are to my taste, but not as television icons, since I am an iconoclast – I can see that they are well and truly celebrated and famous and for all the wrong reasons in my opinion. To find somebody celebrated and famous for the right reasons is no easy task these days!

Probably, this was always the problem with icons, not that it was ever discussed in the early days of religion, outside religious circles.

But one can see from the *Mail's* celebrity list that royals – and not least Queen Elizabeth II – have much more competition than previously in order to get into people's hearts and minds by keeping a high iconic-profile on tele', which is why it is so remarkable that the British monarch has been able to do this for so long and with continuous success. And with far fewer gaffes than others in her family, including those highly-publicised gaffes of her husband, the Duke of Edinburgh, her sexually scandalous sons Andrew and Charles, and her grandson Harry with all the nightclub gossip about him and his wearing a Nazi swastika at a Windsor Castle party, etc, etc.

No doubt traditional royalists and many of the fans of royalty in Britain are outraged that Queen Elizabeth and members of her family – of all people! – should have to sink so low in order to compete with the nation's celebs to get a look in on television, or that they should in any way be compared with them, but, like it or not, that is how the cookie crumbles on television and under the new aristocracy of celebs. This is a new aristocracy that is promoted by television – and by the likes of Piers Morgan in the *Daily Mai*l, he who is himself a television celeb.'

As Piers Morgan has noted in his *Daily Mail* selection 'there are a lot of famous people, many of whom have no right to be,' as well as 'Z-list wannabes scrabbling for their 15 minutes of recognition on increasingly degrading reality-TV shows, desperate for fame of any kind.' So it's time 'to sort the chaff from the wheat,' he reckons, as he gives us his personal selection of the Top I00 famous people in Britain.

But these are arguably people who are mostly famous for being famous, rather than for any kind of public service, or for the *importance* of what it is that they do. They are talented people who have won fame and stardom for whatever it is that they do, rather than for the importance of what they do for the greatness number of people (however many millions follow TV-icons, the greater number is the millions more who do not).

Because there is no attempt to analyse and assess the importance of being a footballer, model, pop singer, musical or other entertainer, talent show presenter or judge, and so on, and the good that this does, these iconic statuses are, to my mind, meaningless.

But, then again, being famous merely for being famous – and celebrated merely for being celebrated – is the name of the game with the new aristocracy these days. Not that there is anything new about this, because many of the old aristocracy once upon a time, had no right to be famous or privileged aristocrats either, they just were, as of birthright, or on account of having friends in the right places to pull strings for them.

They were just a different class of people and maybe they had more class (depending on your taste). But in those days there was no television to expose them or turn them into in-your-face media celebrities. Most average people were not particularly aware of what was going on or who most of them were, and they did not have millions of viewers to 'approve' them. They got by without too much public approval and with just a handful of untelevised people in all the right places, pulling strings for them and opening doors for them (easy peasy!).

One difference between the old and new aristocrats is that the former were monumentally snobby and out of favour with the masses therefore, whom they generally despised, whereas today's new aristocrats is no such thing, or if they are, they keep it to themselves. Snobbery, today, is suicidal for celebs and royals alike, which is why the princes William and Harry are trying to cure themselves of it. The common touch is what counts, but how common does it need to be?

No doubt royalists and fans of royalty (and a goodly number of others besides) find all this tasteless.

But if monarchs and their heirs are to stay close to their people and win their approval for increasing their fan base for their own survival, they are having to undertake a goodly number of tasteless and questionable exercises that they would not have considered for one moment back in history once upon a time, and sometimes they are having to demean themselves.

With television and the Fourth Estate so powerful in the 21st century, the boot is on the other foot now – British royals can no longer ignore the power of television or afford to be condescending to it or distant from it.

Long gone are the days when the trio of the first three estates of government, royalty and church, could treat the media's fourth estate as if it were a secondary outsider.

Whilst Buckingham Palace will still be accustomed to deference inside royal circles and behind the palace gates, it can no longer expect it outside the palace gates, or on the nation's television screens anymore.

Probably it can get it from royalists, but not from royal fans who want a monarchy without the traditional deference shown to it.

When talking of royalists and royal fans, I have in mind for the former, those members of the old school (a dying breed) that consider themselves born to their royalist attachment to the monarchy. Born without even having to think about being royalists, or having to watch a single moment or hour of television (smelly vision!), and who definitely do not consider themselves as fans therefore. Nor do they consider their monarch as a 'celebrity' in any shape or form because she (or he previously) is so much loftier and more worthy and important than that.

But, for the latter fans of royalty, I have in mind those people who watch lots of 'lowly' television, including its tasteless programmes and celebs, but are still fans of royalty for all that, but want their royals to change and be more accessible and more ordinary, more like celebs than royals.

As for the republicans, they are another story (as we shall see in chapter ten).

But even among those who are in favour of royalty there are drastically different attitudes and states of mind, as we shall see in the following chapter, which is why the British public's support of royalty cannot be taken for granted anymore, as it certainly could back in 1952 when Elizabeth came to the throne.

Chapter Nine

Attitudes to Britain's Television Queen

As already mentioned, attitudes to Queen Elizabeth and the British monarchy vary tremendously between different members of the public (and different types of television viewer therefore), and we have heard and seen them all, right throughout her 60-year reign.

If monarchy is to survive in Britain it will depend on the very different attitudes taken by very different members of the British public for different reason, which is why those who care about this matter – for or against royalty – are engaged in a battle to win hearts and minds, for and against royalty. These are campaigning republican and royalist groups who are out to win people to their cause (they also include a goodly number of politicians, for or against royalty)

But, to complicate this issue, there really is a wide divergence of opinion and attitude about this matter.

To begin with, there are people who think that British monarchs and their monarchies are morally/ethically wrong in principle - however harmless, popular or semi-popular they may be - and should be abolished on principle therefore, as some kind of moral and/or republican duty. They regard the monarchy as outdated, the extravagant expense of which can be and should be put to better use. These people exist in each of the political parties including the Conservative party, very probably, that does not necessarily have the copyright on royalist sympathies, although there are very likely more royalists and fans of royalty to be found there than in the other parties.

But then there are others who think that the British monarchy touches the most deeply-felt roots and spiritual and other values of what it means to be essentially British and that interfering others should stop trying to stop them from being British by turning them into republicans. Those of this persuasion are, as we might expect, staunch royalists and loyalists and almost certainly worshipful, religious and Christian, believing in the divine right of kings and queens in some cases, and also in the tribal and ritualistic symbolism and dignity of royalty, together with its patriotism that is near-sacred to them, working as some kind of cultural and racial safety valve against things that are un-British. They really do see the royals as keeping them and the rest of us, including the politicians, on the straight and narrow. They regard monarchy as the most successful form of government and the monarch as a model of character and deportment, capable of gaining the kind of respect for authority and the highest offices of state that politicians can never achieve (they may even be sick and tired of politicians!). These are not only upper-class royalists in the professions and society at large – as well as in the officer class of the armed forces – but working-class ordinary soldiers, sailors and airmen with a strong commitment to the defence of the realm. There are also working-class others who regard the monarchy as the best hope for an orderly and respectful society. Even though they were not 'born' to it, they believe in it. It is no exaggeration to say that all these royalists are under the magic spell of the British monarchy.

But then there are others again who think that fairy-tale kings and queens in the modern world are plain daft –

an insult to modern intelligence – and should be abolished for that reason alone. They are not so much interested in the political pros and cons between republicanism and monarchy, which do not interest them. They simply think that monarchy is too ridiculous and silly for words and should be discontinued therefore in a grown-up society.

There are also those who think that the British monarchy is a peculiar consequence and encumbrance of British history that is relatively harmless these days and can be lived with on account of our history, because it would be too much bother and trouble to dismantle and get rid of it, for as long as it plays its part in paying its way, and for as long as substantial number of people are in favour of it still, as they are entitled to be in a free society (also for as long as the royals behave themselves and do not get too big for their boots). For as long, also, as the royals remain a class act, people of this persuasion regard it as a colourful part of Britain's historical furniture that also furnishes the minds of a sufficient number of people for it to be left alone, and to die a death by its own hand if that is what it is going to do, or otherwise to stay alive and well by its own hand, in the fullness of time They probably think that there is no guarantee that a republican state would be any better (or worse) than a monarchy, or that the disputed cost would be better spent elsewhere, or that they have a moral or any other kind of duty to get rid of an institution such as monarchy that a substantial number of people clearly want, however mistaken or deluded they may be, much of the time. Those of this persuasion are neither royalists/fans of royalty nor republicans, but neutral and disinterested observers rather. They may even enjoy royal pageants and festivities as good fun, attending and celebrating them in the same way as, for example, they attend and celebrate

Chinese New Year. They may even agree that royalty is a *grand illusion*, in the sense that it either is or is not ordinary and does or does not achieve what it is supposed to achieve. On the one hand they believe that royals are born as ordinary people, just like the rest of us, but on the other hand they know that, being royals, they can ever be ordinary like the rest of us! Probably they think that royals cannot survive if they become too ordinary, that there is no point in having a very ordinary royal family. If royalty is a *grand illusion*, like so many other illusions in this world - so what? -is what they say to that. But what they do not believe in, is the rightness of republicans and anti-royals, to sweep aside the sentiments of those who are in favour of royals, not in a free country.

Others again – not republicans, but communists and/or national socialists maybe – believe that royalty stands for outrageous privilege, inequality and an insufferable class system that has no place in a classless society, and is a shocking and wicked expense that cannot and should not be tolerated (unless as a Nazi fascist-monarchy in the opinion of some national socialists who might support it for that reason only).

There are also those who consider themselves to be pragmatists and argue in favour of royalty because they believe that it makes good business sense to keep it on account of the millions of money-spending tourists that it attracts to the UK and because of the international business contracts that are signed with Britain on account of, they believe, royal state visits and Prince Andrew's recent globe-trotting on behalf of British business. Those who think that royalty is plain daft also think that this argument is plain daft, not that those who consider themselves pragmatists ever listen to them.

Then there are the cheep and cheerful fans of royalty, who are by no means staunch royalists, but who like it just the same, because they regard it as English as fish and chips, or as William Shakespeare if you like, not that they ever go to see a Shakespeare play or film, but they do eat plenty of fish and chips!

In short, there are endless very different reasons given by different people for keeping or not keeping the British monarchy and, as we see, this is a very emotive and psychological issue that I have attempted to fathom in this chapter to clarify the matter.

Attitudes swing one way and another like a weather vane!

This royalty issue is a matter of endless speculation about whether Britain will or will not keep faith with its monarchy and its royals and for how much longer.

It is also a matter of endless fascination and even entertainment and amusement to foreign tourists and visitors who wonder about the British and their attitudes to royalty.

My guess is that British monarchy will remain alive and well for the foreseeable future and perhaps even longer (unless it manages to shoot itself in the foot for any reason in some spectacular fashion). On balance, enough people at the top end of politics, the church, the civil service, society and the military, still seem to regard it as an orderly and unifying force for good that keeps us all in our place, as well as a powerful means of promoting national identity and patriotism, keeping us safe from turmoil and revolution, and from presidents and prime ministers from getting too big for their boots (yes, that's what a lot of people still seem to think!).

In the same way that British royalty has evidently taken the view of television – if you cannot beat them, join them – it seems that most in Britain will continue to take the same view of British monarchy and join its cause in one way or another, for one reason or another, rather than seeking to get rid of it.

But one thing on which we can all agree is, presumably, that whatever else may be said about the British monarchy, it is never boring!

Chapter Ten

Is British Royalty Good Value for Money?

Nobody knows whether or not British royalty is good value for money and the reason for this is that a proper cost estimate has not been done.

Those in favour of royalty have not done the estimates properly and those against royalty have not done them properly either.

A blind eye is turned to different costs, depending on whether one is trying justify the total cost or not, as a result of which estimated and/or guesstimated costs are disputed, and included or not in the final tally.

Those against royalty reckon that the costs are much higher than claimed by those in favour of it.

So it is not possible to say in this book – or elsewhere - whether British royalty is or is not good value for money.

The matter is further complicated by what one regards as 'good value' and for what purpose.

Obviously, different people value royalty – like most other things – very differently, depending on their perception of value to the nation and/or society.

Even so, opposing parties have strong views about British royalty being good or bad value for money.

Almost everybody in favour of royalty in Britain today – more than 50% of the population at least and perhaps as many as 80% – will answer yes to the good-value question in the heading of this chapter.

Obviously, British royalty is frightfully expensive, so tax-payer expense has always been a political issue.

Even the royals' greatest fans are generally in favour of plenty of financial scrutiny and constructive financial criticism, with the exception, perhaps of a minority of die-hard royalists.

After all, how can fans of royalty argue that British royals do a good job and are worth the money, if they do not know what the costs are of all the different things that they do?

Because British royals have their hands in the taxpayers' cookie jar year-round, twelve months per annum, it stand to reason that their subjects need to know what these moneys are being used for and whether they are necessary, not least during these hard recessionary times in which we are all having to struggle during Queen Elizabeth II's Diamond Jubilee Year.

It is frequently argued that republicanism is a lot cheaper than monarchy which can no longer be afforded in Britain, which is why costs have become a serious issue and a big stick with which republican and other critics can beat the royals.

You don't have to be a republican to be concerned about this issue, even royalists and fans of royalty may wonder about whether they are getting value for money.

It beats a goodly number of us why the royals did not step in and pay for their own royal yacht when it was decommissioned on grounds of cost, and I was reminded by the decommissioning that, when I interviewed the late Jacques Cousteau in his Paris home, back in the 1970s, he as good as told me that Prince Philip the Duke of Edinburgh was footing the bill for his highly expensive high-tech yacht.

Whilst he would not name Philip, he said that without the support of a high-ranking member of the British royal family with a naval background (so it had to be Philip), he would not be able to afford his yacht that was being used for environmental and underwater purposes on the high seas.

A naval officer himself, Cousteau was a great fan of Britain and British royalty, having lived with his family in Torquay during World War Two, and he is today buried among the great and the good in the Notre Damn Cathedral in Paris.

In view of Prince Philip's World Wild Life and marine environment interests and duties over several decades, it would be surprising if he could not have found a way of funding Jacques Cousteau's yacht. It would be no less surprising if he and the royals could not have afforded to fund - or found a way of funding - their own yacht (we are reminded that they did not wish to pay for the repair work at Windsor Castle after the fire there that reportedly resulted from their electrical wiring that was much in need of improvement).

Obviously, any book about Queen Elizabeth II that turns a blind eye to how much she and her family costs British taxpayers, is not doing its job properly, especially a book like this that is rating her as a television queen (the sensitive and controversial issue of monarchy versus republicanism, over what the costs are, comes with the territory of television that reports and discusses this matter).

One of the reasons why Queen Elizabeth II has set out to become Britain's television queen is all too obviously because she and her family are acutely aware of the dissatisfaction and criticisms in many quarters, about the cost of royalty to tax payers, given that this is a subject that is no stranger to the British media, including television.

Last year Buckingham Palace released its own annual report suggesting that the royal family costs a mere £40 million per annum.

But this is an estimate that is strongly challenged by Republic – an organisation that has the aim of replacing monarchy with an elected head of state – an organisation, furthermore, that reckons that the real annual cost to taxpayers is more than five times the palace figure, in the region of £202.4 million (this Republic figure is more than the £195 million required to feed the entire British Armed forces).

Republic claims that figures coming out of Buckingham Palace exclude the cost of round-the-clock security and armed forces protection for all the royals, as well as the local authority costs for royal visits. With the Queen undertaking an estimated 444 official engagements per annum and all the other royals, including minors, some 2,566 official engagements, the question is bound to arise as to whether the public needs so many royal engagements and whether it is getting good value.

When it comes to the costs of the Duchy of Cornwall and Lancaster estates – thus far excluded from the royal purse – Republic takes the view that we would all be better off if the royal family paid for its own estates (which it claims are not the personal property of the House of Windsor but held in trust for it).

For sure, a lot of money could be saved by taking these estates away from royalty and handing them back to the nation, in order to benefit the nation financially. Without doubt a traditional culture of secrecy and former deference surrounding the House of Windsor has ensured that the British public has hitherto been kept in the dark about these matters.

But not so these days, when the news hounds are around!

With increasing transparency about these and so many other royal matters on television and in the media in the 21st century, Elizabeth II and her family are by no means always given an easy ride. They may be easy riders, but it does not follow from this that they are given an easy ride in the media. On the contrary, they are frequently in the line of fire.

But fortunately for Britain's television queen, she does not, as yet, have to be interrogated by the likes of Jeremy Paxton on *Newsnight*!

However, the time may come when she and other royals will have to do precisely that if they are to survive, as more and more of their mystique is stripped away, as Queen Elizabeth IIs' advisors warned her that it would be, back in 1953 if she did not distance television.

Even British MPs in the House of Commons are up against a long-standing parliamentary convention no to ask too many questions about the monarch and the royal family. This is because there is, for some mysterious reason, an exemption to the Freedom of Information Act applying to royals that makes it very difficult indeed for politicians and the general public to find out anything in the official papers relating to British monarchy.

Graham Smith, campaign manager of Republic, describes British royalty as 'a colossal waste of public money.' He says that every year 'we go through the charade of palace press officers telling us what great value the monarchy is.'

Of course, where one stands on this issue depends on how one feels about public moneys, many of which are, alas, wasted too much of the time in all sorts of ways, and in some cases on a grander scale than they are allegedly being wasted on royalty; which is why, to make the waste of money argument stick, we need a very precise comparison of all the other alleged wastages of public moneys, including London's Olympic Games this year, for example.

We need to compare the big royal family spend – and it is, as Republic rightly points out, massively bigger than its own official figures suggest – with other big spends, such as the Olympics, high-speed rail links that may or may not be strictly necessary, extra airports and so on.

We also need to remember that many people could not care less about wasting public moneys on things of which they approve, only on those of which they do not approve!

We need a televised debate on what is and is not a waste of money and how much it matters to how many people?

We are told by the national tourist agency – VisitBritain – that royals bring in an estimated £500 million per annum in tourism alone, but do we seriously believe that most tourists would not come to Britain in the absence of its royals and Buckingham Palace and the other royal residences?

Then there is the argument that royals are supposedly helping Britain to win orders abroad for British products, which seems unlikely, given that so many other nations are winning more orders than Britain and without any royals!

Royals may be eye-candy for foreign businessmen, foreign governments and foreign tourists, but it doesn't seem likely – doesn't it? - that they are the reason for people abroad doing business with Britain, or coming to visit Britain.

Then there is the value and cost of the self-worth that is supposed to come from being proud to be British, which is what the royals are supposed to enable people to be, not least with all their costly pageantry, military tattoos and the like.

But, when we consider the antics of Prince Andrew, for example, and all his helicopter flights and his ex-wife's (Fergie's) well publicised claim - caught on camera by an undercover journalist - that he was perfectly aware of her attempts to sell access to him at £500,000 per time!, well how proud can we or other royals feel about that?

No wonder he goes ballistic when such things get into the press and on television.

This gives rise, in turn, to the perfectly legitimate question about whether royals, such as Prince Andrew or

Fergie, should be sacked for such activities, and if so whose responsibility this should be!

With or without being republicans, we need to ask these and so many other questions about British royalty and not take no for an answer, which is why I am giving a fair hearing to Republic's financial arguments and figures in this book.

Republic are the only people regularly and seriously challenging the royals' official figures and not infrequently ridiculing them.

In this life we all *pays our money and takes choice* – unless we live in a dictatorship – and let's not forger that there are plenty of republics that are more expensive and less accountable than British monarchy.

In its history, Britain had its chances for revolution and getting shot of its kings and queens, but has not taken them, so getting shot of royalty today seems rather irrelevant and too late to a great many people.

But this is not to say that British monarchy should not pay its ways much more than hitherto and stop making excuses for not putting its rich hand in its deep pockets.

What British royalty is particularly good at is showing the flag at home and abroad and, for as long as people flag wave and rally round the totem pole, why discontinue it for those that like it?

But at what price?

Whilst all this may be all very peculiar to the critics of royalty, peculiar is not against the law, is it?

If peculiar is how people are – how the human condition is – why should we, how can we, ban it?

When all is said and done, what the masses want is what they get, and they get the television and the royalty they deserve, the cost of which may or may not interest them very much.

So we see, once again, why it is in the interests of Queen Elizabeth II to have a big presence on television, as Britain's television queen, if she and her monarchy are to win favour rather than lose it and to survive in the foreseeable future.

For maximum effect, they need to win the cost argument, not least on television.

Chapter Eleven

Rites of Passage for Britain's Television Queen

It is no exaggeration to say that television, for Queen Elizabeth II, has been the introduction to a new world of some very strange *rites of passage* from 1953 right through to her 212 Diamond Jubilee.

During this period she has made the transition from one societal and televised status to another and another, taking to the high seas on a long journey in which she has crossed the equatorial line in more ways than one.

One can say this metaphorically (and also literally on some occasions).

These television rites were very strange to her when she first had the crown placed upon her head in front of the cameras, because she went, as a complete stranger, to where no royals had been before, into the world of television, and became a changed and very different person in the process.

By the same token, her monarchy changed as well, because it of course lost much of its mystique, as it was bound to do, as a result of the journey that she took, as she gradually became of age as Britain's television queen.

No doubt she will not have realised or been aware of the rites in question, because no historians have suggested or recorded them before, which is perhaps hardly surprising, given that rights of passage on television bring a whole new understanding to the traditional meaning of ancient rites, as Elizabeth and others will have understood it.

It is when we solemnise or celebrate life-changing or developmental events that they are called rites in the English Language, meaning a solemn ritual, which in turn means a serious procedure or procedures, regularly followed in order to highlight the procedure or procedures in question. And seeing as we can do this without any religious or spiritual attributes these days, then not all rites have to be religiously inspired or solemnised, as many people perhaps think. There are such things as secular rights also and it is these secular rites of which we can speak where Queen Elizabeth II's television rites are concerned.

Television for has been a baptism of fire - rather than of holy waters - from which she has emerged largely victorious, dampening the flames in some cases (as in the aforesaid case of Princess Diana's funeral) and putting them out in others (as in the case of the royal scandals of her children, from which she and the media have moved on), ever since she crossed the line, back in 1953.

Crossing the line – the equatorial line – is a rite of passage made by sailors who have travelled from West to East, from one world to another, to become of age and to become changed seamen in the process, and when Queen Elizabeth travelled from the dark world of radio with its largely unseen monarchy, into the new and forbidden, bright new world of television - against which she was warned because of the perceived threats and dangers there (to her royal mystique) - the heat was well and truly on as she crossed the line in a very profound and significant way. That was her first right of passage.

The phrase *baptism of fire* (*or by fire*) has been used in the English Language in the modern sense since the early 19th century when it arrived on British shores in translation from the French - *bapteme du feu* - referring to the first experience of soldiers under fire and it is certainly true that Queen Elizabeth was under fire from her advisors when she underwent her baptism on television at her coronation in 1953 as Britain's newly-crowned television queen, before being under fire from television in the fullness of time for not living up to the public's expectations during the Princess Diana controversy.

Whilst there are also biblical origins and meanings for *baptism of fire*, it is the modern meaning with which we are concerned here, just as we are concerned with the modern societal meaning of *rites of passage* and not its spiritual meaning, on the television journey that she has taken.

As we can clearly see, the ceremonial ritualisation of Queen Elizabeth's coronation on our television screens in 1953 - for the entire world and her homeland to see and for the first time in royal and television history - marked the beginning of a new journey for her in more ways than one. It was then that she was born and baptised, as it were, as Britain's television queen. It was then that in terms of the societal implications of television, she was but a child with much to learn before she became of age, as she experienced some typical rites of passage to do with her personal development and changed identity.

Concepts of rites of passage have bee around since the beginning of time to mark the transition between childhood and full inclusion into a tribe or social group, impacting on anthropological thought thereby, and also on religious thought in view of the spiritual aspects not infrequently attributed to different concepts.

But one does not have to be religious - as Queen Elizabeth certainly is - to recognise, ceromonise and ritualise the important changes in our lives that help to guide us on our way, changing our lives as we go.

This has happened to Elizabeth at the televising of her coronation, of her first televised Queen's speech on Christmas day, and her first reality-TV programme, each event of which has turned her into a television queen and sent her on her way into the next stage of her journey.

There are three *rites of passage* here, in addition to the aforementioned crossing the line right.

With or without attributing any spiritual or religious connections or implications to these life-changing events that we call *rites of passage*, we are all generally aware of how they can affect our growth and development, linking the individual to the community in a new secular or religious context (if in the latter, then we are talking about linking the individual not only to the community but to the spiritual world beyond and maybe to an afterlife).

Whilst we cannot attribute any spiritual role to Queen Elizabeth's television *rites of passage*, we can certainly attribute a secular and societal role to them, because her television journey has affected her non-spiritual growth and development and linked her to the community and the big wide world in no uncertain way – a new and very different way, changing her image and also the traditional type of monarch that she would otherwise have been had she decided to have no truck with television, as she was advised to do when the first came to her throne.

We can also attribute ceremonial rites to this in the sense that when millions of people turned on their television sets to watch her coronation, and repeatedly watch her thereafter, including her Queen's speech every Christmas day, year after year, and then to watch her reality-TV show, they were of course ceremonialising and ritualising her in their homes, as they had done previously when they watched her coronation at the outset of her journey.

Nothing spiritual about this, but *secular rites of passage* indeed, and nothing uncommon or new about these rites being secular, given that there are so many others besides, of which the following are but three examples.

When young men join the armed forces they have traditionally been given a sharp haircut, to remind them that they have been 'cut away' from their mothers, their homes and their former civilian lives and given a new identity as potential fighting men in the making (I remember my first army haircut only too well, back in 1959, when I was conscripted into the British Army to do my National Service) and, for sure, Queen Elizabeth II was sharply cut away from British monarchy's former untelevised life when she let the cameras into Westminster Abbey to show her coronation in 1953 (albeit without having her hair cut!).

Another secular example is to be found in Canada where graduating engineers have marked their *rites of passage* within their profession, symbolised by an iron-ring that is supposed to bond them all together as young engineers and make them conscious of the significance and responsibilities of their profession, directing their consciousness and pointing them in a new direction with expressions (or oaths) of intention to that end.

Whilst Queen Elizabeth II has made no expressions of intention, or taken any oaths, as Britain's television queen, she has not needed to, because the very act of allowing the previously forbidden cameras into Westminster Abbey said it all. The implications and the new responsibilities were obvious in those early days of television when there was a very clear equatorial line between two very different worlds – the new transparent world and the old secretive and mysterious world of royalty.

The old world was pre-occupied with an ancient mystique that did not allow for televised coronations, or even speeches, or Christmas Day speeches, let alone monarchs in reality-TV programmes, all rites of incorporation and societal inclusion, incorporating the British monarch in a new way with her people, as opposed to the monarchical exclusion that had existed previously.

Even the Duke of Edinburgh's Outward Bound courses are potential *rites of secular passage* for young people participating in his adventure education programmes that are designed to advance the young on life's journey and to turn them into outward bound individuals who are hopefully more adult and mature in consequence, after they have been prepared for life's challenging journey.

So, as we see, there's no shortage of *non-spiritual* or *secular rights of passage*, and I am clarifying this because people who have been brought up on *spiritual and/or religious rites of passage*, may not clearly understand that rites can also be non-spiritual and secular. They may not understand that one can 'solemnise' ritualistic rites in ways other than the spiritual and/or the religious.

In different cultures and countries, rites of passage take many different forms across the globe from – to mention but a few - coming of age (the key of the door), bar mitzvah and circumcision to baptism, cutting of the sacred cord, pilgrimage, born again, sacred bonds of incorporation, marriage, college/university graduations, debutante balls, ancestorship, vision quest and so on.

Where television is concerned, it has been a television quest for Queen Elizabeth.

But whilst the outward symbols and conceptions of *rites of passage* have varied, most of the passages/journeys in question have been conceived and structured in three parts to get us through life's journey, from birth and childhood to adulthood, and then to a gradual and final understanding and completion of who were are. This has been the common pattern in most countries and cultures, although there is no reason why one cannot have more than three stages of development, as and when appropriate.

In this chapter a three or four stage development has been suggested for Queen Elizabeth as Britain's television queen, tracing the journey that she has taken into the world of television.

She has gone from the televising of her coronation in 1953, which was her first rite of separation - separating her from the previous status of untelevised monarchs in the days of radio and from those who did not approved of a televised coronation - followed by a second transitional stage in which she was suspended between statuses, and also by a third when she crossed the line with reality-TV – and finally by her fourth and final rite of aggregation when her new status as television queen was conferred. When we think about it, this kind of trajectory in life applies to most of us in one way or another, but in the case of the Queen of England it certainly applies to her relationship with television with her steady graduation towards qualifying as Britain's television queen.

Her second transitional stage in which she was suspended between statuses took her to the first televising of her Christmas Day's Queen Speech after her coronation, leaving the public to wonder where she might go to from there as she was held in suspension until she took the next step into the world of reality-TV, whereupon she had gradually become a very changed person and a very different kind of queen.

Whilst her *rites of passage* are not generally referred to – because they are not generally understood – they are an important part of her story as Britain's television queen, which is why they are explained in this chapter.

Without them she would not have become the popular queen that she has become, and the reasons for her popularity are the subject of the following chapter, reminding us that, providing she did not swim against the television tide, she could hardly fail to be popular.

Chapter Twelve

Reasons for the Queen of England's Popularity

The reason why the Queen of England remains continuously popular with the British public – with 50%-plus to 80% popularity ratings – is, I would suggest, chiefly because she is non-political.

When public figures are non-political, it's not difficult to be popular with people - given that they are agreeable and kindly and have some charm – and this is because they don't actually do anything of a political nature to upset or disappoint people.

By contrast, prime ministers are bound upset and/or disappoint people, sooner or later, simply because they are prime ministers who cannot possibly please most or all of the people, most or all of the time!

Being out of politics makes life a lot easier for British royals, including the Queen of England. All they have to do is to remember not to make waves, or disappoint, and maybe to pour oil on troubled waters behind the scenes, as and when required, but without getting politically involved. As public relations people, fronting for the different governments that come and go, they just have to show a kindly and caring royal face to the public, as of course the Queen of England does.

She does this a lot better than others in the royal family, some of the outspoken comments of whom (her husband, the Duke of Edinburgh, her sons the princes Charles and Andrew, and her daughter, Princess Anne, have indeed made waves from time to time, expressing their irritation with the media, or with architects and architecture (in the case of Prince Charles), and not infrequently behaving in sexually scandalous and other ways! Not that a large slice of the ever-tolerant British public – with a substantial soft spot for royalty still – has not forgiven them for this, because it has, so they too have remained popular, because whatever else they many have done, they have not engaged in every day politics and got up the noses of voters. But they have not done it with the effortless and consummate skill and good grace of Queen Elizabeth II.

It is this skill and good grace that is her greatest asset, coupled with the fact that being non-political, she is not in the line of fire like her prime ministers.

Obviously, if you are not political, you cannot easily offend or annoy people, seriously disappoint them, or let them down, or invite their criticism or prejudice, because they never know where you stand or what you stand for on matters concerning their health, wealth, welfare and jobs.

Because you are not required to show your hand, your people never know if you agree with the financial cutbacks that are losing them their jobs, or that social benefits should be capped, or what you think should be done about the economic recession and the inflated commissions of banker, or about workplace problems, immigration, the health service, education, the economy, homosexual marriages, problems of race, terrorism, abortions, social problems and foreign affairs. And not knowing all this about you, they have no reason to resent you or hate you or feel dissatisfied with you. Because you are neutral and well out of it and their love or respect for you is unconditional, how can you be unpopular? You cannot, unless you do something non-political that gets up their noses?

As we have seen in chapter X, the Queen of England has done this only once, with regard to the late Princess Diana, for which she was forgiven by recognising the error of her ways and convincing her people of this, whereupon she was pretty much instantly forgiven, regaining her approval from them once again.

All things considered, being a British monarch, one is foot loose and fancy free, and there are few banana skins on which to slip up, compared to prime ministers and politicians whose paths are littered with slippery banana skins, and who get ten times more criticism than monarchs or royals, who are far and safely removed from the daily rough and tumble of politics and political argument.

Since people are not looking to monarchs and other royals to show their hands politically, royals cannot really go wrong in the popularity stakes, because they are not responsible for everything that goes wrong when it goes wrong, as are prime ministers whose popularity sinks like a lead balloon for these reasons!

Whilst it seems reasonable to suppose that the Queen of England, being a monarch, is likely to be very conservative, we have no idea if she is a political conservative therefore, and even if she is, she has the advantage of nobody knowing this and taking against her for it – as left-wing and liberal people do – because she never says anything in favour of the conservative party to draw their criticism or make her unpopular with all those who are politically anti-conservative.

Ditto religious affairs.

We hear that she is a good Christian who believes in God and we know that she is the figurehead of the protestant Church of England, but because she is not required to say anything in favour of Christianity at the expense of the other religions, or even at the expense of atheists in her country, she can remain popular, therefore, with Catholics, Jews, Muslims, Hindus and all the other religions, because she never says anything to make herself unpopular with them.

If people knew what she really thought politically, racially or religiously and what she really stood for, they might not like her as much as they do, so better by far that they do not know, that they are kept in the dark about her. From time to time, they have heard gaffes from her husband, the Duke of Edinburgh, on the subject of 'slitty-eyed' Chinese and 'electrically wiring that looks as though it was done by Indians' (not these days, but no matter!), but never any such gaffes from her, so they can only wonder about her and what she thinks racially and/or politically.

If she were not the Queen of England, would she be a Thatcherite Tory or a new-look Cameronite, in favour of a Coalition government, or a liberal and socialist perhaps?

Who knows?

Nobody knows, or cares, given that she has not political role to play.

All she needs to do is to be a good and caring, kindly mother or grandmother to her people and her own family, and she will remain forever popular in the eyes of those with whom she is popular. For as long as she does this with charm and good grace, and does not become too remote, she cannot lose. She will always have the approval of her fans.

What she does not need to do, with her winning smile, to be an arrogant, petulant, irresponsible, remote or undutiful royal, which she never is.

For all these reasons, she is a carefree easy-rider who can never be to blame when things go wrong – as prime ministers and politicians can – because it is all too obviously not her fault, which is why of course she is blameless.

Given that most people look for hate-figures that they can seriously hate – not just among politicians but celebrities as well, and also among different religious sects, among business and professional people and so on – the Queen of England knows very well that there is no chance of her ever becoming a hate figure, as long as she carries on doing what she is doing, never putting a foot wrong, and doing what she does best, better than all the other royals put together.

For all that most people know, if British royals were prime ministers and/or government ministers instead of being non-political royals, they might be even worse than those that are prime ministers and government ministers, but most people will never know this or perhaps even suspect it if they are staunch royalists (I have actually heard some royalists say that they would rather have royalty running the country than democratically elected politicians!).

Against this background it is apparent that being a monarch is not in the least difficult. All one has to do is serve one's country in a decent non-political way, and play one's part as it is prescribed. Whilst prime ministers and politicians may be thrown to the lions, monarchs never will.

All one has to do is to remember the rules of the game and keep a careful eye on one's easy popularity with the people. Being a British monarch must surely be one of the best and easiest jobs in the world, the rewards and satisfactions of which are second to none (on wonder a lot of commoners and nobles want to marry into the British royal family!).

I am not suggesting that there is anything wrong with this, or that British royals should change their ways, because they certainly should not.

This chapter is only to explain the reasons why it is easy for our royals and Queen Elizabeth to be popular and why Elizabeth should carry on doing what she has been doing so well for 60 years now, seeing as she is a lot more popular than previous monarchs in recent history, and may yet prove to have been more popular than those who succeed her.

In fact, as we see in this chapter, she is pretty much a perfect model of dutiful and caring perfection for the consideration of future monarchs, taking care not to be petulant or arrogant, or too remote from or too near to her people - to common or uncommon - and to remain tight-lipped and discreet at all times, steering well clear of politics and political comment, and keeping her thoughts and her own judgement to herself.

Of course, after 60 years on the throne, she has had plenty of admirable practise, and this certainly shows, and long may it continue.

In the final chapter of this book, we can see how popular the Queen of England and other British monarchs have been, precisely, in my view, because they are non-political and have remained that way.

Chapter Thirteen

Different Audiences for Television Queen

We have seen in these pages how television has helped to make Queen Elizabeth II and how, in turn, she has helped to make it.

But the audiences for her programmes have been changing drastically throughout her 60-year reign, which is why she and her family have been struggling to keep up with these changes, with which they have judged that they cannot afford to be left behind, if they are to be a modern royal family in a modern society.

These days, formality is definitely out for most TV programmes about royalty, whilst informality is in.

Having embraced television at the time of her 1953 Coronation, it stands to reason that she needs to embrace the changes that it has brought with it, if she is to continue as a credible television queen.

Without doubt, Queen Elizabeth and television have been a mighty big help to each other, finding different audiences for each other from which both have benefited hugely – Elizabeth increasingly projecting her image to her people, with a view to keeping them on side, and the television channels attracting more viewers thanks to her.

But there has also been a dumbing down on television, which raises the question and the problem for British royals: how far should they – can they afford to – dumb down?

Some people take the view that they can dumb down as much as they like in order to remain popular with their people, many if not most of whom seem to love dumbing down at every opportunity!

If the British monarchy is to continue to be good for television business, as it has been - whilst television is to carry on being good for keeping the monarchy upfront in the minds of its people, finding new audiences for it is probably a must.

The royal family may or may not employ audience research specialists at Buckingham Palace – on confidentiality contracts (we shall never know) – but with or without them it has a shrewd eye for what is going on, on the box, and how to keep up with it.

We have Prince Charles' wife, Camilla, the Duchess of Cornwall, launching a *Cooking for the Queen* competition for school children during Her Majesty's Diamond Jubilee Year, telling viewers that the monarch has plain taste in cuisine and that, if Camilla were going too cook for Queen Elizabeth, she would probably cook roast chicken!

Some observers have dubbed this competition – which has got instant television news coverage and will doubtless get much more before the Jubilee year is out – a 'cooking for granny' competition.

At this rate, we may even finish up with a royalty TV-cookery programme, showing how different royals cook in their kitchens......

This is but another example of the length to which 21st century royals are going to keep abreast of changing TV-times and changing audiences, on this occasion a children's and schools audience, and perhaps a parents and general interest audience.

But, once upon a time, in the pre-television era – pre 1940s and 1950s, given that the first public service television did not arrive in the UK until 1936 prior to World War Two in 1939, and did not seriously begin to take off until the 1950s – there was virtually only one television audience of which to speak.

This was a very singular and formal upper and lower class audience that was almost entirely royalist, from cloth-cap fans of royalty at the bottom fish and chip end of the spectrum, to the middle and upper classes above them, each sector of which had one thing in common, which was that they were pretty much all fans of royalty who wanted to know more about the royal family and see more of it on television on the terms of the royal family, not theirs – the exceptions were in a minority and there were no seriously critical or anti-royal programmes for them (they came later in and after the 1960s).

As we have seen in this book, Elizabeth and her family have been getting into informal reality-TV and sports quiz-programmes, gardening and other programmes and also showing for the talent-show *X Factor* programme, whilst being involuntarily dragged into *Spitting Image* programmes (grinding their teeth, no doubt!).

However, this single and very formal audience of yesteryear, for Britain's television queen, did not last for too long - with its televised *Coronation*, and its *Christmas Day Queen's Speeches/Messages* every year, and annually televised *Remembrance Poppy Days* on the second Sunday every November, and so on.

And I would suggest that the reason it did not last long was because, when the 1960s and 1970s came along, there was a great sea change in television viewing that lead to a diversity of different audiences for different interests and tastes in the UK, for which very different programmes were coming on stream for the first time in television history.

People who had previously had fewer programmes to watch on tele' suddenly had many more and they soon became spoilt for choice. They were no longer obliged to carry on watching the same old stuff, royal and other traditional, very formal stuff. They also had a different and less obedient approach to royalty from British television that may have caused a lot of families to think again about British royals.

People watching the *Queen's Speech/Christmas Message* halved from an estimated 70% of the population in the 1960s to 35% thereafter, to as recently as some ten years ago by all accounts. But since 2009, the viewing figures have reportedly fallen again for the tried and true old royalty programmes, from 28 million for the *Queen's Christmas Speech* in 1987 to a fluctuation 5/8 million at Christmas time, in recent years.

Yet there are more ways of watching this speech than ever before – *Sky TV*, *BBC*, *ITV* and *You Tube*, but, ironically, far fewer people watching than before!

Obviously there is a need for royalty to retrieve some of this lost television ground.

In the early days, an estimated 150 million tuned into the monarch's Christmas-time speech worldwide, so we can see from this steady decline that viewers have become bored with it and are turned on by - and tuned in to - other Christmas programmes instead.

No doubt the *Queen's Christmas Message* has become old hat in their view and the view of their children and grand children, reminding us that the television queen that moved with the times, has suddenly fallen behind the times in some respects.

For this and other similar reasons, British royalty needs to look elsewhere to keep a regular public profile and positive TV-image in the minds of the people, which is what it has been doing, as we have also seen. If it can no longer command attention in the formal TV programmes of yesteryear, it must identify with other programmes that can command attention, and participate in different programmes of its own, as it has done from time to time.

On *Remembrance Day* - poppy day - Sundays every November, when something to the order of 30 million red poppies are sold, obviously a lot of these poppy wearers are also watching the magnificent poppy-day show on television, of which the Queen of England is the star. This is a great show and, together with the Chelsea Flower Show, this *Remembrance Day* ceremonial is the longest-running live-TV show in the world, with something to the order of an estimated 12 million viewers annually, reportedly.

But this is only once a year, so what to do in the meantime?

But *Remembrance Day* is a memorial history show, not simply a show about the Queen of England sending a brief message – as in her *Christmas Day Speech* – but a show about all the armed forces and civilians that are commemorated in two world wars (WWI and WW2). This is a colourful and fascinating and very dignified TV spectacular, by any standard, for an audience that is different again from the dwindling audience that are falling away form the *Christmas Day Speech* (maybe it is time for the speech to be reformatted and to include some more interesting and less predictable subjects?)

For the British monarchy to feature in some widely-viewed television programmes to make its presence felt, it will need to project itself differently and find different things about it and the story it has to tell, new things that are suitable for new programmes for new audiences, as it has already begun to do, and will have to do more in future.

This is why Queen Elizabeth and her family have been getting into informal reality-TV and sports quiz-programmes, gardening (Prince Charles at Highgrove) and other programmes, and also 'showing' for and identifying with the talent-show, *X Factor*, whilst being dragged into *Spitting Image* programmes (grinding their teeth, no doubt!), and letting it be known that Her Majesty likes and follows *Downton Abbey*.

From the point of view of winning the favour of the greatest number of people - and potential royalty fans thereby - the choice of *X Factor* and *Downton Abbey*, at opposite ends of society and the market, is a shrewd one that strikes an interesting and remarkable balance.

X Factor is the biggest TV talent show in Europe with a staggering 19.7 million viewers in the UK (63.2%) of audience share, 10 million votes from the British public, and some 200,000 auditionees. With these viewing figures, this is a programme that even royalty cannot afford to ignore.

By contrast, the *Downton Abbey* period costume-drama, written by Julian Fellowes, has a very respectable 10 million viewers in the UK and another 1.6 million in the United States, and it has entered this year's *2012 Guinness Book of Records* for being the most critically acclaimed English-language TV-show since *Brideshead Revisited*, back in 1981. With two series under its belt already, a third is coming later this year.

So, from just two very opposite and very different shows and audiences, one posh and the other not, we have 29.7 million viewers in the UK whose favour can perhaps be won by the Queen of England by letting it be known that she shares her people's enthusiasms for both these programmes, as well as their tastes and enjoyment of such shows.

Normally, most people who enjoy *Downton Abbey* would not be seen dead watching *X Factor*, but the Queen of England is not most people!

And she doubtless has reasons of her own for identifying with the shows that she identifies with.

Ditto all other 'favourite' programmes that we read that the British monarch is said to watch.

But it's not only that people are more spoilt for choice on television these days that they are no longer watching the *Queen's Speech* at Christmas, and other similarly formal programmes.

It is also, in my opinion, because of the great television satire boom in the 1960s, notably as a result of David Frost's *That Was the Week That Was*, as well as *The Pythons*, of course, in addition to other programmes besides, by such stars as Pete and Dud (Peter Cook and Dudley Moore) and the Australian comedian, Dadaist and satirist, Barry Humphries (of *Edna Everidge* fame), he who was at *The Late Show* in those days.

I knew these people at that time and was occasionally involved with them, having written a script for a new television programme to be called *Smelly Vision* for the late Spike Milligan, who tried to get it on air, but was turned down by the BBC (he wrote to me 'sorry I tried').

Probably the BBC did not like my visualising and satirising a situation in Britain in which the Tory MP and government minister, the late Enoch Powell, was supposed to be running his own Big Brother television station, selling television sets from which the on-off knobs had been removed, so that people could not turn their sets off!

The comedian Spike Milligan liked my script but the BBC apparently were less than enthusiastic about the idea!

It was the white racist, passionately anti-immigrant Enoch Powell, who had made his infamous 'rivers of blood' speech back then, that was widely reported in the media, but for which he was dismissed from the Conservative cabinet by its leader, Prime Minister Edward Heath (predictably, Powell had also been a supporter of the racist apartheid government in South Africa that was denying the blacks their rightful independence and their country, keeping Nelson Mandela from power).

Times really were changing radically and swiftly for Queen Elizabeth and her subjects, as was British television.

I also knew Barry Humphries and the master of satire, Peter Cook in those distant times, with the latter of whom I had some boozy and informative meeting in local Hampstead Village restaurants in North London, and for the former of whom I wrote some verse poetry for an anthology of Australian verse that Barry edited for paperback publication in Australia under the title *Innocent Austral Verse* (published by Sun Books in Melbourne).

Barry asked me to respond to current events in the 1960s, with long verses about the war in Vietnam, Sir Francis Chichester's round the world yacht race from Sydney to the UK, and with an elegy of the Tasmanian bush fires, which I wrote from press cuttings and television news reports.

When I went to visit him and his first wife in their grand home – in London's Little Venice – he mischievously told me 'I know you're not Australian, but I like your work so much that I am making you into an Australian by adoption and will refer to you as an Australian living in London in the Earl's Court Road!'

I have never been to Australia in my life or lived in the Earl's Court Road!

Later on, I got to know John Cleese, with whom I corresponded for a several years, after interviewing him in the 1970s in his palatial Holland Park home for a feature that he wanted to get on the coloured cover of *Marketing Week* (of which I was the business editor, after moving on from *The Times* newspaper), when he was selling his management-training film company.

When I interviewed John - over a plate of very tasty French cheese and dry white wine - he had just left his first wife, the delightful Connie Booth, who had acted with him in *Fawlty Towers,* and he had moved her into a palatial villa, very similar to his own, just down the street.

These were fun times for very clever and talented fun people, as a result of which television was becoming a lot more fun, with more people on and off the television screens poking fun at British royalty, among other institutions, and to its credit, British royalty has generally gone along with this, not least Queen Elizabeth.

The point about my own experiences here is that I knew quite a few of the notable pioneers in Britain's television satire boom and how they were thinking, whilst they were liberating British television from its previously lofty formality and the deference that had been customarily shown to the British establishment, including British royalty naturally.

Many new people – chiefly out of the universities of Oxford and Cambridge if they were British - were openly questioning and challenging royalty, much more than previously, and generally waking viewers up to the idea that maybe they did not need royalty anymore, or if they did, not in the same old formal way in which it had been presented to them. For the first time in television history there was an attack on hypocrisy and traditional thinking wherever it was found, and all were targets, including the royals.

All this satire was opening the eyes of millions of television viewers to the shortcomings of governments and of various hallowed and pompous institutions, including the church, the law courts and the monarchy, as well as the class system that propped up the monarchy and many other institutions besides.

It was the kind of televised satire that one could only get in England and it was being pioneered in London.

A great wave of amusing, witty and disrespectful satire swept across the nation and swamped our television screens, which is why the groundbreaking *That Was the*

Week That Was alarmed an easily alarmed establishment so much that the programme was sadly discontinued (there has been nothing like it since). It was on this programme that the late *Time's* journalist, Bernard Levin got punched by a male member of the audience for having criticised his actress wife in a newspaper article. He asked Bernard to stand up and then knocked him down in front of 10 million television viewers in 1963! Bernard Levin recovered and carried on, as before, asking his studio audience if he could continue on a non-violent basis, for which he got a big round of applause.

Bernard Levin (and I) were with *The Times* newspaper before Rupert Murdoch got his hands on it, the *Times* being the 'top people's' paper (which it no longer is), of which Bernard seemed to be destined to be editor in the fullness of time, long before Murdoch came along decades later, to upset Bernard's applecart, having got the approval of Prime Minister Margaret Thatcher (her government ignored the monopoly laws in his favour).

When *The Times* was eventually sold to Murdoch, was when I and other journalists moved on, because we did not like the idea of working for an increasingly powerful, monopolistic and interfering publisher, and events vindicated our mistrust of him and his growing power, as we now know from the government's current Leveson Enquiry into his publishing affairs. Whilst I continued to freelance for *The Times* after it had been sold to Murdoch, on business and legal matters, I did not come under his direct control or methodology, or the control of his lackeys.

In addition to the 1960s satire boom on British television – like nowhere else in the world - there were also the satirical print publications in London – *Oz* and *Private*

Eye - the latter owned by Peter Cook and for the latter of which I wrote some pieces and got to know its journalists, including the late Paul Foot, the great pioneering investigative journalist in the UK, who once told me over the phone, with regard to a fellow *Eye* journalist who did not have Paul's home telephone number, 'whatever you do, don't give him my number, because he is completely mad,' and there were indeed some zany journalists on the *Eye* who were metaphorical mad.

At a lunch with the *Eye*, in a local Soho pub, I sat next to the Catholic journalist, Mary Kenny, who had to listen to my irreligious and atheistic views, as we both sat opposite editor Richard Ingrams and his late deputy, Auberon Waugh (son of the famous literary novelist Evelyn Waugh), who moved on to launch and edit *The Oldie*, after Peter Cook had appointed Ian Hislop to succeed Ingrams.

It is said that Hislop's appointment put Auberon Waugh's nose out of joint, which is why he left the *Eye* in a huff to join Ingrams.

As noted previously, Ian Hislop, an unknown quantity back then, has now become a television icon or sorts, with his own TV fans and after dinner speeches, fans who like his brand of humour and satire (yet another very different television audience).

With the shape and face of British television changing so drastically, with so many new and different kinds of audience coming on stream, we can see that the monarchy has its hands full if it wants to keep up, as it has shown every sign that it does.

It is against this evolving background, that it is perhaps hardly surprising that republicanism had been growing in the UK throughout this period, probably as a result of both the right-wing and left-wing sectors of the British press becoming much more questioning and openly critical of the conduct of a goodly number of royals, as well as questioning the expense of royalty – such questioning and criticism would never have been openly expressed in the media during pre-television times – all of which has been reflected on our television screens, almost certainly becoming of growing concern to old-style royalty.

Any Buckingham Palace public relations advisor worth his or her salt – and there are several press officers at the palace – would have been telling the royal family that it needed to counter its loss of popularity of not quite half the population, by boosting its appeal in new ways for different television audiences, if it wanted to hang on to slightly more than half the population (some 52% in favour or monarchy).

If the younger royals could not clean up their act, then at least make them and Queen Elizabeth more popular with all sorts of people in all sorts of television audiences, to win their favour for other things and in other ways, such as taking part in the aforementioned comic *It's A Royal Knock Out* show, sports quiz-programmes and the like, including (perish the thought!) reality-TV programmes and showing for *X Factor*.

The time had come for the Queen of England and her family to get into a new-look television era and cut some new mustard.

Regardless of whether the royals liked it or not, the time had come for them to identify with these programmes in some way and/or to let it be known that they watched them and liked them, in order to relate to their people and win their approval.

By paying attention to all these different television audiences, Britain's television queen has massively increased her chances of getting millions of new fans from all sorts of very different programme in different social sectors in terms of quality, taste , or otherwise of not losing her existing fan base.

But some of these programmes are decidedly down market (but with massively greater viewing figures than the other upmarket programmes).

The heir apparent, HRH Prince Charles, gave permission for film footage of him talking to *Coronation Street's* fictional Audrey Roberts, to be incorporated in the fictional storyline of this working-class television soap opera, in which a real-life Charles was shown on a Coronation Street television screen talking to Audrey.

Throughout the *Corrie* series, mildly and quaintly snobby Audrey, is supposed to have been distantly related to royalty (or so she has told everyone), and now she is suddenly talking to Prince Charles, having been presented to him as a local council dignitary at the Weatherfield Council on a visit made to the council by the prince.

But, in reality, the film footage came from Charles making a royal visit to Manchester in the year 2,000 and turning out for *Coronation Street's* 40t anniversary, by visiting its Manchester-based television studios and meeting the *Coronation Street* cast, before returning to London.

Again we see how royals identify with television programmes and their audiences.

With viewing figures fluctuating from 16 million to 27 million throughout its lifetime, *Coronation Street* is a widely watched TV-soap, with some 9.3 million watching at the last count in 2012. Like all figures given for TV programmes, there is some confusion and mismatch between millions of homes, as opposed to the actual number of viewers who live in the homes (which may be a higher figure), but *Corrie*, together with *East Enders*, is ahead of the field in the long-running TV-soap genre.

Whether we shall see Queen Elizabeth turning out for a television soap opera during her Diamond Jubilee year remains to be seen!

Chapter Fourteen

Prominent People and the Queen of England

Because the British monarchy is the longest-surviving governmental institution in Britain and Europe - it is hard to escape British royals in history, as we shall see in this chapter. Because British monarchs and their courts have been around for such a very long time indeed, it is hardly surprising that they have attracted a lot of historical attention from historians as well as from elsewhere, from media commentators, politicians and authors, all of whom have had a lot to say on the inevitable subject of British royalty throughout the ages, and so it seems fitting to conclude this book with some highly favourable quotes about royalty from the Constitutional Monarchy Association (CMA) in London.

These quotes are taken from its website, at its invitation, because they really are too good to miss, and they are reproduced here in order to end this book on a light but thought-provoking note − a celebratory note in view of this year's Diamond Jubilee celebrations.

The CMA reports that it has been collecting these quotes from different sorts of people to 'spice up an argument or garnish a school essay about British royalty,' and as we can see, in the opinion of many prominent people, British royalty is a hard act to follow.

There are all sorts of perceptive and amusing quotes here, as follows;

If a nation does not want a monarchy, change the nation's mind. If a nation does not need a monarchy, change the nation's needs.

Jan Christian Smuts, Prime Minister of South Africa 1939-1948.

I am a true servant of my King and country, not only as a dutiful subject, but because I am a convinced monarchist, politically and intellectually. I mean by that, quite apart from myself and my relationship to my Bavarian and German fatherland, I believe monarchy to be the most successful form of government that the history of mankind has known.

Adolf von Harnier, on trial for treason, Germany 1938.

If the Allies at the peace table at Versailles had allowed a Hohenzollern, a Wittelsbach and a Habsburg to return to their thrones, there would have been no Hitler. A democratic basis of society might have been preserved by a crowned Weimar in contact with the victorious Allies.

Winston Churchill, 26th April 1946.

In Italy they are already speaking about a republic, but keep in mind that there is nothing less suited to Italians...... The Italians are individualists and a republic will become the cause of confusion and disorder. Certainly of corruption. I have no doubt of it. When all this comes to pass who will profit from it?

King Victor Emmanuel III of Italy, 10th April 1944.

(King George VI) represented, for us, a model of character and deportment for those in high places. Our respect for him as an inspirational force was equalled by our affection for him as a gentle human being.

General Dwight D Eisenhower, 7th February 1952.

This war would never have come unless, under American and modernising pressure, we had driven the Habsburgs out of Austria and the Hohenzollerns out of Germany. By making these vacuums we gave the opening for the Hitlerite monster to crawl out of its sewer on to the vacant thrones. No doubt these views are very unfashionable....

Winston Churchill, 8th April 1945.

The public are sick and tired of politics, they are sick and tired of the machinations of elected office in a media age, and I think it's quite good having a Head of State that's completely to one side of that.

Simon Upton, New Zealand Environment Minister, March 1994.

I notice that the constitutional monarchies are the most democratic countries of Europe. I can't understand how there could be any debate about it.

Jack Lang, French Minister of Culture, October 1993.

If constitutional monarchy were to come to an end in Britain, parliamentary democracy would probably not survive it. It is, after all, through the monarchy that parliamentary control over the armed forces is mediated and maintained.

Conor Cruise O'Brien, The Independent, 25th June 1993.

I am personally still convinced that there are safeguards in the constitutional monarchy that an elected head of state just would not possess.

Roger Stott MP, The Independent on Sunday, 7th September 1997.

The Prince of Wales, as so often, has demonstrated his common sense in the words he spoke on Wednesday (during his visit to southern Africa). His demeanour is a perfect illustration of the benefits of a constitutional monarchy. In the heat of euphoria, in the midst of all the blather about a "new" this and a "new" that, his is a message of modernisation and wisdom. We would do well to heed it."

Kwasi Kwarteng, The Daily Telegraph, 31st October 1997.

Anyone who fears that by becoming a republic we would condemn ourselves to a presidency held by a perpetual succession of superannuated politicians - at the moment presumably a choice between Heath, Kinnock, Thatcher and Major - is an optimist. The alternative nightmare scenario looks not to the European model but to the American, where the essentials for election to the presidency appear to be ruthless ambition, access to vast wealth, reckless promises of patronage and preferment, effective control of a big slice of the media and a plausible TV manner. We don't know when we are well off.

Gordon Medcalf, The Independent, 10th September 1997.

I write by the light of two eternal truths: religion and monarchy, those twin essentials affirmed by contemporary events, and towards which every intelligent author should seek to direct our country.

Honore de Balzac, 1842.

Monarchy is the one system of government where power is exercised for the good of all.

Aristotle, 322-384 BC.

Being a nation of hypocrites, we have for years looked to the Royal Family to embody the values we're not prepared to embody ourselves.

Serena Mackesy, The Independent, 10th December 1996.

Why has destiny willed the downfall of this Sovereign? He is endowed with every kingly quality; he is courageous, generous, and magnanimous; he has a fine intellect and a well-balanced mind; and his name bears the tradition of a thousand years of history. Who better than he to symbolise the unity of the country, and act as supreme moderator in party strife?

> Aldo Castellani, Physician to Umberto II of Italy, June 1946.

Those who imagine that a politician would make a better figurehead than a hereditary monarch might perhaps make the acquaintance of more politicians.

> Baroness Thatcher, November 1995.

Thus the young royals are reproached for setting a bad example and failing to keep their marriages together by journalists who themselves lead Casanova-like lives.

> Richard Ingrams, The Observer, 31st March 1996.

Canadians should realise when they are well off under the Monarchy. For the vast majority of Canadians, being a Monarchy is probably the only form of government acceptable to them. I have always been for parliamentary democracy and I think the institution of Monarchy with the Queen heading it all has served Canada well.

> Pierre Trudeau, Prime Minister of Canada, 1973.

If to be a Republican is to hold, as a matter of theory at least, that is the best government for a free and intelligent people in which merit is to be preferred to birth, then I hold it an honour to be associated with nearly all the greatest thinkers of the country and to be a Republican. But if a

Republican is one who would thrust aside the opinion and affront the sentiment of a huge majority of the nation, merely to carry to a logical conclusion an abstract theory, then I am far from being a Republican as any man can be.

Rt Hon Joseph Chamberlain (1836-1914) in 1875.

The State functions more easily if it can be personified. An elected President who has stepped out of politics, like the French President, is no substitute for a King who has stepped in by right of inheritance. Still less is an active politician, like the President of the United States, a substitute. We can damn the Government and cheer the King.

W Ivor Jennings, The British Constitution, 1943.

Modern monarchs neither have nor need executive power. Integrity and continuity are their stock in trade. These qualities are becoming more precious when European political parties, many of them in power for a decade or more, are increasingly judged arrogant or corrupt or both. Politicians could with profit learn not to treat modesty as merely a royal prerogative.

Editorial, The Times, 2nd August 1993.

The monarchy is a political referee, not a political player, and there is a lot of sense in choosing the referee by a different principle from the players. It lessens the danger that the referee might try to start playing.

Earl Russell, The Spectator, 11th January 1997.

I think it is a misconception to imagine that the monarchy exists in the interests of the monarch. It doesn't. It exists in the interests of the people.

HRH Prince Philip, Duke of Edinburgh, 1969.

The fact that the Monarchy can unify in this way - can comfort and exhilarate and embrace - remains, as Cameron (James Cameron, republican journalist) put it, its great 'gesture to all the forces of logic', the power before which the neat rationality of republicanism wilts.

Robert Harris, Mail on Sunday, 7th September 1997.

For any country it is better to have a monarch than an elected president of the republic ..... monarchies provide the continuity of states, while prime ministers come and go. Elections are all very well for the designation of the prime minister or of the party which should take power, but not for the Head of State, who should be above party.

(Unlike a president) in all probability the monarch who succeeds to the throne has been trained for this exalted post by having spent many years by the side of his predecessor.

A monarch, however, cannot declare that he is ready to throw in his hand. The personal conveniences of sovereigns are of little importance. What is important is that Great Britain needs them.

George Brown (Foreign Secretary in the Wilson government), Daily Mail, November 1969.

The Royal tour (of South Africa) gives reassurance that when it comes to flying the flag nobody does it quite as well as the Queen.

The Guardian, 22nd March 1995.

A priest who is not a monarchist is not worthy to stand at the altar table. The priest who is a republican is always a man of poor faith. God himself anoints the monarch to be head of the kingdom, while the president is elected by the pride of the people. The king stays in power by implementing God's commandments, while the president does so by pleasing those who rule. The king brings his faithful subjects to God, while the president takes them away from God.

Neomartyr Vladimir, Metropolitan of Kiev, tortured and killed by Bolsheviks on 7th February 1918.

The Queen was helpful, lively, fascinating to talk to, and very, very funny. The idea that she is out of touch is nonsense.

Robert Wraith, painter of Her Majesty's portrait, May 1998.

The monarchical principle is laughed at by vulgar and foolish people in all the suburbs of Europe. It is hated in all the gutters of the world. The reason is simple. It enshrines with a fitting dignity and elaboration the principle of authority as something independent of this or that politician. It places it above attack. It symbolises and consecrates an attitude of mind essential to the happiness of peoples.

D'Alvarez, Storm Over Europe, by Douglas Jerrold (1930), Chapter XII.

The British love their Queen, their Queen Mother, Prince Charles, and the comforting security of their hereditary constitutional monarchy, an institution of which the characters are beyond the manipulation of man, an institution guaranteeing continuity, overriding the dissensions of politics. The best governments are constitutional monarchies, and we may yet see some restored in eastern Europe.

Lord Menuhin, The Daily Telegraph, 2nd July 1998.

In republics there is not a respect for authority, but a fear of power.

Dr Samuel Johnson (Boswell's Life, p 464).

The best reason why Monarchy is a strong government is that it is an intelligible government. The mass of mankind understand it, and they hardly anywhere in the world understand any other.

Walter Bagehot, The English Constitution, 1867.

I think the family has got to streamline itself but the core members have a brand personality that a business would die for. You might say they're the brand identity of

Britain: ask any American what they'd give to have a Royal Family.

Jack Stevens, advertising agent, The Independent, 30th June 1998.

Above the ebb and flow of party strife, the rise and fall of ministries, and individuals, the changes of public opinion or public fortune, the British Monarchy presides, ancient, calm and supreme within its function, over all the treasures that have been saved from the past and all the glories we write in the annals of our country.

Sir Winston Churchill.

To be a king and wear a crown is more glorious to them that see it than it is a pleasure to them that bear it.

Queen Elizabeth I.

Parliaments and Ministers pass, but she abides in lifelong duty, and she is to them as the oak in the forest is to the annual harvest in the field.

William Gladstone, writing about Queen Victoria.

Russia under Nicholas II, with all the survivals of feudalism, had opposition political parties, independent trade unions and newspapers, a rather radical parliament and a modern legal system. Its agriculture was on the level of the USA, with industry rapidly approaching the West European level.

In the USSR there was total tyranny, no political liberties and practically no human rights. Its economy was not viable; agriculture was destroyed. The terror against the population reached a scope unprecedented in history.

No wonder many Russians look back at Tsarist Russia as a paradise lost.

Oleg Gordievsky, letter to The Independent, 21st July 1998.

Americans also seem to believe that the monarchy is a kind of mediaeval hangover, encumbered by premodern notions of decorum; the reality is that the British monarchy, for good or ill, is a modern political institution - perhaps the first modern political institution.#

Adam Gopnik, The New Yorker, September 29th 1997.

I consider tolerance as one of the ruler's first duties. I have always tried to be tolerant and to respect and treat with consideration all kinds of religious beliefs. In this respect the ruler must not permit any discrimination. During my long reign in Bulgaria there was no persecution of those belonging to another faith, of Mohammedans or Jews. Had there been any I would have punished those responsible with the greatest severity.

Ferdinand I, King of the Bulgarians (Abdicated 1918), 1931.

Be the person in relation to whom .... all things in your Kingdom are ordered; the person in whom your people perceive their own nationhood; the person by whose existence and dignity the national unity is upheld".

General de Gaulle in a speech addressed to Queen Elizabeth II.

We should all bear carefully in mind the constitutional safeguards inherent in the monarchy:

While the Queen occupies the highest office of state, no one can take over the government. While she is head of the law, no politician can take over the courts. While she is ultimately in command of the Armed Forces, no would-be dictator can take over the Army.

The Queen's only power, in short, is to deny power to anyone else. Any attempt to tamper with the royal prerogative must be firmly resisted.

D G O Hughes, letter to The Daily Telegraph, 1st September 1998.

I have always been vaguely comforted by the sense that the Crown, and therefore the nation, endures like weathered granite through whatever turpitude and buffoonery may pass in Parliament. There is also something re-assuring in the knowledge that every Prime Minister, every week, has a confidential and not necessarily comfortable conversation with a monarch: that is to say with someone who is not their dependant, not their sycophant, who has no political affiliation beyond patriotism and who has seen governments rise and fall over decades. This sense of continuity, of a nation mature enough to be able to make electoral mistakes and later recant without risk of losing its identity, is profoundly useful.

Libby Purves, The Times, 8th September 1998.

A Republic of Great Britain Bill would dominate the lifetime of a parliament to the detriment of all other economic and social affairs, and if passed would change virtually every facet of British life beyond recognition. From postage stamps to the names of warships, every area of political, social, economic, financial, religious and civil life would be transformed, and potentially unleash political forces beyond our control or comprehension.

Paul Richards, in the Fabian Society pamphlet Long to reign over us?, August 1996.

There is no doubt that of all the institutions which have grown up among us over the centuries or sprung into being in our lifetime, the Constitutional Monarchy is the most deeply founded and dearly cherished.

In the present generation it has acquired a meaning incomparably more powerful than anyone had dreamed possible in former times. The Crown has become the mysterious link, may I say the magic link, which unites our loosely bound but strongly interwoven Commonwealth of Nations, states and races. People who would never tolerate the assertions of a written Constitution which implies any diminution of their independence are the foremost to be proud of their loyalty to the Crown.

Winston Churchill, February 1952.

Kings have advantages over democratic politicians. Although they must remain popular ..... they do not have to grub for votes. Unlike American senators, they are not obliged to start raising money for their re-election campaign days after the electorate has voted them in. Inheritance has its privileges, for both rulers and the ruled......For politicians in democracies, the business of government is all too often a great game, a chance to strut and posture their little moment on the stage, before retiring to directorships and lecture tours. No such retreat is possible for monarchs, so they are less likely to mess with the dodgy loan, or fool around with the intern.

Editorial, The Spectator, 13th February 1999.

The monarchy's most important constitutional function is simply to be there: by occupying the constitutional high ground, it denies access to more sinister forces; to a partisan or corrupt president, divisive of the nation; or even to a dictator. The Queen's powers are a vital safeguard of democracy and liberty.

Sir Michael Forsyth, speech 26th January, 1999.

This country suffered greatly as a result of the abolition of the monarchy in 1970. We support it, because it is an institution the country needs, for its unity and its development.

There is a Cambodian proverb which says "While you are eating fruit, don't forget who planted it."

We must not forget our King and his vital role in securing a victory for democracy in our country. If he had not remained here during the elections, or if he had not personally appealed to our citizens to vote, the population would without doubt have been afraid to participate and we would not have achieved the 90% turn out that we did. And perhaps the international observers would not have agreed to come."

Hun Sen, Prime Minister of Cambodia, July 1998.

For every monarchy overthrown the sky becomes less brilliant, because it loses a star. A republic is ugliness set free.

Anatole France, first winner of the Nobel Prize for Literature, 1921.

My grandfather was of peasant stock and I am prouder of that than of my throne. Crowns are lost, but the pure blood of those who have loved the earth does not die.

King Peter I of Serbia.

Parliamentary monarchy fulfils a role which an elected president never can. It formally limits the politicians' thirst for power because with it the supreme office of the state is occupied once and for all.

Max Weber, German economist.

Anyone who has walked through the deserted Palaces of Versailles or Vienna realise how much a part of the life of a nation is lost when a monarchy is abolished. If Buckingham Palace and Windsor Castle were transformed into museums, if one politician competed against another for the position of President of the Republic, Britain would be a sadder and less interesting place. Our politicians are not men such as could challenge more than a thousand years of history!

William Rees-Mogg, former Editor of The Times.

[A] king is a king, not because he is rich and powerful, not because he is a successful politician, not because he belongs to a particular creed or to a national group. He is King because he is born. And in choosing to leave the selection of their head of state to this most common denominator in the world - the accident of birth - Canadians implicitly proclaim their faith in human equality; their hope for the triumph of nature over political manoeuvre, over social and financial interest; for the victory of the human person.

Jacques Monet, Canadian historian.

It is helpful when the personality of the head of state is not disputed or contested periodically. The monarch is the incarnation of popular hope and the repository of national legitimacy.

Henri, Comte de Paris (1908-1999).

No practising politician could possibly hope to be more deeply and widely informed about domestic, Commonwealth and international affairs than The Queen. She has sources of information available to nobody else.

James Callaghan, British Prime Minister 1976-79.

Not to be a republican at 20 shows lack of heart. To be one at 30 shows lack of head.

Francois Guizot, French statesman 1787-1874.

Most Australians - contrary to what is constantly claimed - are not yet republicans. The Queen, touring the country with dignity at this slightly touchy time, says that she sees herself as the servant of the Australian Constitution and of the people. It is fair to suggest that many of Australia's republican leaders do not quite see themselves as so answerable.

Geoffrey Blainey, The Age, March 2000.

I had been told the Queen is not interested in anything political and speaks only on social issues. On the contrary, the Queen is very well informed on a number of international issues and on security matters.

Vladimir Putin, Russian president-elect, 18th April 2000.

All of us who come here [to the UK] do so because the notion of Britishness is far more than merely ethnic - or at least we think it is. You may not go on about it as much as Americans do, but you also have a set of ideas attached to your national identity, and we admire them. We most admire, in fact, those bits of your national identity which you seem most keen on discarding: not just boring old political liberty and economic freedom, which we could get in America or lots of other places, but history, tradition, centuries of stability, tolerance of eccentricity, cars which drive on the wrong side of the road, flat green lawns and, above all, a Queen, together with her Heirs and Successors. After spending the first part of my life being a mere citizen, I am delighted to find myself a subject as well.

Anne Applebaum (on becoming a British subject), The Spectator, 6th May 2000.

I don't think I really came to appreciate what royalty meant to you Brits until I came to Wimbledon, with all its pomp and circumstance. It is tradition, it is such an important factor here and you start thinking it's not bad when you see the effect it has on people. I suppose the monarchy is a bit like grass at Wimbledon. How long will it last? My guess is that they will both go on for many, many years to come.

John McEnroe, The Sunday Telegraph, 2nd July 2000.

I have previously observed that British republicans seem to have a blind spot about the family: they do not grasp that the Royal Family touches some chord in most of us linked with family feeling. Even as an Irishwoman, I feel a warm sense of maternal protectiveness when I pass Buckingham Palace and see the Royal Standard flying. The Queen is at home, and a benign matriarchal wisdom prevails over the land.

Mary Kenny, The Daily Telegraph, 1st July 2000.

Also from MX Publishing

Featuring some stunning and rare pictures of Queen Elizabeth II this heartwarming autobiography from John Jochimsen comes from one of the last people left alive who were there at the moment her father died and Elizabeth became queen.

John Jochimsen, 80 Years Gone In A Flash.

www.ingramcontent.com/pod-product-compliance
Lightning Source LLC
Chambersburg PA
CBHW071701090426
42738CB00009B/1619